Make Ahead
CLASSICS

RDA ENTHUSIAST BRANDS, LLC
MILWAUKEE, WI

94

48

54

Make Ahead
CLASSICS

EDITORIAL
EDITOR-IN-CHIEF Catherine Cassidy
VICE PRESIDENT, CONTENT OPERATIONS
Kerri Balliet
CREATIVE DIRECTOR Howard Greenberg

MANAGING EDITOR, PRINT & DIGITAL BOOKS
Mark Hagen
ASSOCIATE CREATIVE DIRECTOR
Edwin Robles Jr.

EDITOR Hazel Wheaton
GRAPHIC DESIGNER Courtney Lovetere
LAYOUT DESIGNERS Nancy Novak,
Catherine Fletcher
EDITORIAL SERVICES MANAGER Dena Ahlers
EDITORIAL PRODUCTION COORDINATOR
Jill Banks
COPY CHIEF Deb Warlaumont Mulvey
COPY EDITORS Dulcie Shoener (senior),
Ronald Kovach, Chris McLaughlin, Ellie Piper
CONTRIBUTING COPY EDITORS Michael Juley,
Valerie Phillips

CONTENT DIRECTOR Julie Blume Benedict
FOOD EDITORS Gina Nistico; James Schend;
Peggy Woodward, RDN
RECIPE EDITORS Sue Ryon (lead), Irene Yeh
EDITORIAL SERVICES ADMINISTRATOR
Marie Brannon

CULINARY DIRECTOR Sarah Thompson
TEST COOKS Nicholas Iverson (lead),
Matthew Hass
FOOD STYLISTS Kathryn Conrad (lead),
Lauren Knoelke, Shannon Roum
PREP COOKS Bethany Van Jacobson (lead),
Melissa Hansen, Aria C. Thornton
CULINARY TEAM ASSISTANT Maria Petrella

PHOTOGRAPHY DIRECTOR Stephanie Marchese
PHOTOGRAPHERS Dan Roberts, Jim Wieland
PHOTOGRAPHER/SET STYLIST
Grace Natoli Sheldon
SET STYLISTS Melissa Franco (lead),
Stacey Genaw, Dee Dee Schaefer
SET STYLIST ASSISTANT Stephanie Chojnacki

**BUSINESS ARCHITECT, PUBLISHING
TECHNOLOGIES** Amanda Harmatys
**BUSINESS ANALYST, PUBLISHING
TECHNOLOGIES** Kate Unger
**JUNIOR BUSINESS ANALYST, PUBLISHING
TECHNOLOGIES** Shannon Stroud

EDITORIAL BUSINESS MANAGER Kristy Martin
RIGHTS & PERMISSIONS ASSOCIATE
Samantha Lea Stoeger
EDITORIAL BUSINESS ASSOCIATE
Andrea Meiers

EDITOR, *TASTE OF HOME* Emily Betz Tyra
ART DIRECTOR, *TASTE OF HOME* Kristin Bowker

BUSINESS
VICE PRESIDENT, GROUP PUBLISHER
Kirsten Marchioli
PUBLISHER, TASTE OF HOME Donna Lindskog
**BUSINESS DEVELOPMENT DIRECTOR,
TASTE OF HOME LIVE** Laurel Osman
**STRATEGIC PARTNERSHIPS MANAGER,
TASTE OF HOME LIVE** Jamie Piette Andrzejewski

TRUSTED MEDIA BRANDS, INC.
PRESIDENT & CHIEF EXECUTIVE OFFICER
Bonnie Kintzer
CHIEF FINANCIAL OFFICER Dean Durbin
CHIEF MARKETING OFFICER C. Alec Casey
CHIEF REVENUE OFFICER Richard Sutton
CHIEF DIGITAL OFFICER Vince Errico
**SENIOR VICE PRESIDENT, GLOBAL HR
& COMMUNICATIONS**
Phyllis E. Gebhardt, SPHR; SHRM-SCP
GENERAL COUNSEL Mark Sirota
VICE PRESIDENT, PRODUCT MARKETING
Brian Kennedy
VICE PRESIDENT, OPERATIONS Michael Garzone
**VICE PRESIDENT, CONSUMER MARKETING
PLANNING** Jim Woods
**VICE PRESIDENT, DIGITAL PRODUCT
& TECHNOLOGY** Nick Contardo
**VICE PRESIDENT, FINANCIAL PLANNING
& ANALYSIS** William Houston

COVER PHOTOGRAPHY
PHOTOGRAPHER Grace Natoli Sheldon
FOOD STYLIST Kathryn Conrad
SET STYLIST Dee Dee Schaefer

© 2017 RDA ENTHUSIAST BRANDS, LLC.
1610 N. 2ND ST., SUITE 102, MILWAUKEE WI
53212-3906

INTERNATIONAL STANDARD BOOK NUMBER:
978-1-61765-676-7
LIBRARY OF CONGRESS CONTROL NUMBER:
2017930992

COMPONENT NUMBER: 116000225H

ALL RIGHTS RESERVED.

**TASTE OF HOME IS A REGISTERED
TRADEMARK OF RDA ENTHUSIAST
BRANDS, LLC.**

PRINTED IN CHINA
1 3 5 7 9 10 8 6 4 2

PICTURED ON THE FRONT COVER:
Wintertime Braised Beef Stew, p. 38

PICTURED ON THE BACK COVER:
Blueberry Quick Bread with Vanilla Sauce, p.101;
Favorite Chicken Potpie, p. 63; Chicken Florentine
Meatballs, p. 58

PICTURED ON THE TITLE PAGE:
Marmalade Meatballs, p. 17; Peanut Butter Cream
Pie, p. 103; Cuban Ropa Vieja, p. 41

99

Make family meals that fit your schedule!

Today's busy cooks take advantage of a host of **time-saving strategies** to make sure they don't miss out on **home-cooked meals for the family**. Recipes prepared the night before, slow-cooked classics made in the morning and ready at mealtime, or tasty dishes made during downtime and frozen for a weeknight meal—all give time-pressured cooks lots of options.

Taste of Home Make Ahead Classics delivers **151 great recipes** that make the most of plan-ahead tricks. Savory staples, sweet treats, sides, appetizers...they're all freezer-friendly, made in the slow cooker or prepped ahead of time. Recipe-specific tips for freezing ensure that every dish is as delicious when you serve it as when you made it. Hearty mains like **Sirloin in Wine Sauce (p. 46),** tasty appetizers like **Moroccan Empanadas (p. 16),** mouthwatering morning meals like **Baked Blueberry-Mascarpone French Toast (p. 85)** and stunning desserts like **Butter Pecan Cheesecake (p. 105)** are all within easy reach.

Keep an eye out for special icons that highlight recipes throughout the book. SLOW COOKER 🍲 dishes will cook while you're busy doing other things, and (5)INGREDIENTS recipes call for five or fewer ingredients (not counting staples like salt, pepper and oil). Watch for high-yield recipes (check the index on p. 109 for a list!) and assemble two or more dishes at once—one for dinner tonight, and the others to stock the freezer!

Take the pressure off of a hectic work week by knowing you have a dish of **Chicken Manicotti (p. 61)** at your fingertips. And if unexpected guests drop in, why not pull out a loaf of **Lemon Pound Cake (p. 99),** or a batch of **Swiss & Caraway Flatbreads (p. 13)?**

Each recipe was tested and approved by the *Taste of Home* Test Kitchen, so you're sure to have success with every recipe you choose. Yes, you can serve up delicious, homemade suppers even **when your time is tight!**

101

12

37

24

52

76

TABLE OF CONTENTS

27

LOOK FOR THESE HANDY ICONS:

SLOW COOKER
Set it and forget it! Assemble the recipe in the morning, and come home to a simmering dinner from the slow cooker.

⑤ INGREDIENTS
With the exception of water, salt, pepper and oil, these recipes call for only a few items, many of which you probably already have on hand.

DISCOVER MORE MAKE-AHEAD CLASSICS ON TASTEOFHOME.COM

GET SOCIAL WITH US!

LIKE US
facebook.com/ tasteofhome

PIN US
pinterest.com/ taste_of_home

FOLLOW US
@tasteofhome

TWEET US
twitter.com/ tasteofhome

To find a recipe
tasteofhome.com

To submit a recipe
tasteofhome.com/submit

To find out about other
Taste of Home products
shoptasteofhome.com

EASY APPETIZERS

Having party appetizers made in advance means you can spend more time with your guests as they arrive! For a quick snack—in the afternoon or the middle of the night—nothing's better than having tasty tidbits in the freezer, ready to go!

MOROCCAN EMPANADAS, P. 16

MEDITERRANEAN TOMATO BITES

MEDITERRANEAN TOMATO BITES

My friend Mary served these lovely appetizers at a summer gathering, and I adapted them to my taste. It's a great August recipe when tomatoes and herbs are at their freshest.

—SUSAN WILSON MILWAUKEE, WI

PREP: 20 MIN. • **BAKE:** 15 MIN.
MAKES: 32 APPETIZERS

- 1 package (17.3 ounces) frozen puff pastry, thawed
- 1½ cups shredded Gouda cheese
- 6 plum tomatoes, thinly sliced
- ¼ cup pitted ripe olives, coarsely chopped
- 1 cup crumbled feta cheese
  Minced fresh basil
  Minced fresh oregano

1. Preheat oven to 400°. Unfold puff pastry. Cut each sheet into 16 squares; place squares on parchment paper-lined baking sheets.
2. Sprinkle with Gouda cheese; top with tomatoes, olives and feta cheese. Bake until golden brown, 14-18 minutes. Sprinkle with herbs.

FREEZE OPTION *Cover and freeze unbaked pastries on waxed paper-lined baking sheets until firm. Transfer to freezer containers, separating layers with waxed paper; return to freezer. To use, bake pastries as directed, increasing the time as necessary to heat through. Top the pastries as directed.*
NOTE *Puff pastry is convenient, but it's very rich. Lighten up this appetizer using toasted French bread slices. Decrease baking time slightly and skip the freeze option.*

SHIITAKE & GOAT CHEESE RUSTIC TART

Even if you usually prefer sweet to savory, you'll love this tart featuring goat cheese and shiitake mushrooms. Refrigerated pie pastry makes for easy assembly.

—KAREN WATTS CORTLANDT MANOR, NY

PREP: 20 MIN. • **BAKE:** 30 MIN.
MAKES: 6 SERVINGS

- ½ pound sliced fresh shiitake mushrooms
- 2 shallots, thinly sliced
- 1 tablespoon butter
- 1 tablespoon olive oil
- 1 teaspoon minced fresh thyme or ¼ teaspoon dried thyme
- ⅛ teaspoon salt
- ⅛ teaspoon pepper
- 1 sheet refrigerated pie pastry
- 4 ounces fresh goat cheese, crumbled

1. In a large skillet, saute mushrooms and shallots in butter and oil until tender. Remove from the heat; add thyme, salt and pepper.
2. On a lightly floured surface, roll pastry into a 14-in. circle. Transfer to a parchment paper-lined baking sheet. Spoon the mushroom mixture over the pastry to within 2 in. of edges; sprinkle with cheese.
3. Fold up the edges of the pastry over filling, leaving center uncovered. Bake at 375° for 30-35 minutes or until crust is golden brown. Serve warm.
FREEZE OPTION *Freeze unbaked tart until firm, then cover to store in freezer. To use, remove from freezer 30 minutes before baking (do not thaw). Preheat oven to 375°. Place tart on a parchment paper-lined baking sheet. Bake as directed, increasing time as necessary.*

(5)INGREDIENTS

BALSAMIC-GLAZED CHICKEN WINGS

Tired of the same ol' buffalo and BBQ sauces? Try spreading your wings with a balsamic-brown sugar glaze. Sweet and mildly tangy, these have a taste that'll appeal to any crowd.

—GRETCHEN WHELAN SAN FRANCISCO, CA

PREP: 20 MIN. + MARINATING
BAKE: 25 MIN.
MAKES: ABOUT 1½ DOZEN

- 2 **pounds chicken wings**
- 1½ **cups balsamic vinegar**
- 2 **garlic cloves, minced**
- 2 **teaspoons minced fresh rosemary or ½ teaspoon dried rosemary, crushed**
- ¼ **teaspoon salt**
- ¼ **teaspoon pepper**
- ¼ **cup packed brown sugar**

1. Cut chicken wings into three sections; discard wing tip sections. In a small bowl, combine vinegar, garlic, rosemary, salt and pepper. Pour ½ cup marinade into a large resealable plastic bag. Add the chicken; seal bag and turn to coat. Refrigerate for 1 hour. Cover and refrigerate remaining marinade.
2. Drain the chicken and discard marinade; place in a greased 15x10x1-in. baking pan. Bake at 375° for 25-30 minutes or until no longer pink, turning every 10 minutes.
3. Meanwhile, combine brown sugar and reserved marinade in a small saucepan. Bring to a boil; cook until liquid is reduced by half.
4. Place wings in a large bowl. Pour glaze over wings and toss to coat.
FREEZE OPTION *Cover and freeze cooled wings in freezer containers. To use, partially thaw in refrigerator overnight. Reheat wings in a foil-lined 15x10x1-in. baking pan in a preheated 325° oven until heated through, covering if necessary to prevent excess browning.*
NOTE *Uncooked chicken wing sections (wingettes) may be substituted for whole chicken wings.*

FIESTA PINWHEELS

FIESTA PINWHEELS

Whenever I serve these appetizers, they disappear fast. A friend from the office shared them with me, and after one bite I knew I'd be bringing her recipe home.

—DIANE MARTIN BROWN DEER, WI

PREP: 15 MIN. + CHILLING
MAKES: ABOUT 5 DOZEN

- 1 **package (8 ounces) cream cheese, softened**
- ½ **cup sour cream**
- ¼ **cup picante sauce**
- 2 **tablespoons taco seasoning Dash garlic powder**
- 1 **can (4½ ounces) chopped ripe olives, drained**
- 1 **can (4 ounces) chopped green chilies**
- 1 **cup finely shredded cheddar cheese**
- ½ **cup thinly sliced green onions**
- 8 **flour tortillas (10 inches) Salsa**

1. In a small bowl, beat cream cheese, sour cream, picante sauce, taco seasoning and garlic powder until smooth. Stir in olives, chilies, cheese and onions. Spread about ½ cup of cream cheese mixture on each tortilla.
2. Roll up tortilla jelly-roll style; wrap in plastic. Refrigerate for 2 hours or overnight. Slice rolls into 1-in. pieces. Serve with salsa.
NOTE *Pinwheels may be prepared ahead and frozen. Thaw pinwheels in refrigerator.*

**PORK & CHIVE
POT STICKERS**

1 minute. Repeat with the remaining oil, pot stickers and broth. If desired, serve with additional soy sauce.

FREEZE OPTION *Place uncooked pot stickers on waxed paper-lined baking sheets; freeze until firm. Transfer to resealable plastic freezer bags; return to freezer. To use, cook frozen pot stickers as directed, increasing broth to ½ cup and simmering time to 4-6 minutes when cooking each batch.*

NOTE *Wonton wrappers may be substituted for pot sticker and gyoza wrappers. Stack two or three wonton wrappers on a work surface; cut out circles with a 3½-in. biscuit or round cookie cutter. Fill and wrap pot stickers as directed.*

LEMONY FENNEL OLIVES

When spring arrives, I like to prepare recipes with fresh flavor. This make-ahead dish can be served either as an appetizer alongside crackers or as a condiment for a meat entree.

—LORRAINE CALAND SHUNIAH, ON

PREP: 20 MIN. + CHILLING
MAKES: 16 SERVINGS

- 1 **small fennel bulb**
- 2 **cups pitted ripe olives**
- 1 **small lemon, cut into wedges**
- ½ **teaspoon whole peppercorns**
- ½ **cup olive oil**
- ½ **cup lemon juice**

1. Trim the fennel bulb and cut into wedges. Snip feathery fronds; reserve 2 teaspoons. In a small saucepan, bring salted water to a boil. Add the fennel. Boil, uncovered, for 1 minute or until crisp-tender. Drain and rinse in cold water.

2. In a large bowl, combine the fennel, olives, lemon wedges, peppercorns and reserved fennel fronds. Whisk oil and lemon juice; pour over the olive mixture. Toss to coat. Cover and refrigerate overnight.

3. Remove from the refrigerator 1 hour before serving. Transfer to a serving bowl; serve with a slotted spoon.

PORK & CHIVE POT STICKERS

I keep a batch of these potstickers in the freezer; my three kids are old enough to cook them themselves. The hidden veggies in mine make them better than the restaurant's!

—MARISA RAPONI VAUGHAN, ON

PREP: 1 HOUR • **COOK:** 5 MIN./BATCH
MAKES: 5 DOZEN

- 2 **medium carrots, finely chopped**
- 1 **small onion, finely chopped**
- ½ **cup finely chopped water chestnuts**
- ⅓ **cup minced fresh chives**
- 1 **large egg white, lightly beaten**
- 3 **tablespoons reduced-sodium soy sauce**
- ½ **teaspoon pepper**
- 1 **pound ground pork**
- 60 **pot sticker or gyoza wrappers**
- 3 **tablespoons canola oil, divided**
- 1 **cup chicken broth, divided**
  Additional reduced-sodium soy sauce, optional

1. In a large bowl, combine the first seven ingredients. Add pork; mix lightly but thoroughly. Place a scant tablespoon of filling in the center of each wrapper. (Cover the remaining wrappers with a damp paper towel until ready to use.)

2. Moisten the wrapper edges with water. Fold the wrapper over filling; seal the edges, pleating the front side several times to form a pleated pouch. Stand pot stickers on a work surface to flatten bottoms; curve slightly to form crescent shapes, if desired.

3. In a large nonstick skillet, heat 1 tablespoon oil over medium-high heat. Arrange a third of the pot stickers in concentric circles in the pan, flat side down; cook 1-2 minutes or until bottoms are golden brown. Carefully add ⅓ cup broth (broth may splatter); reduce heat to medium-low. Cook, covered, 2-3 minutes or until the broth is almost absorbed and the filling is cooked through.

4. Uncover and cook until the bottoms are crisp and broth has completely evaporated, about

LEMON-MARINATED ANTIPASTO

LEMON-MARINATED ANTIPASTO

This make-ahead recipe speaks to my Italian heart. I like to serve crusty Italian bread on the side to soak up the awesome dressing.
—**NANCY BECKMAN** HELENA, MT

PREP: 20 MIN.
COOK: 15 MIN. + MARINATING
MAKES: 12 SERVINGS (½ CUP EACH)

- 1 package (19½ ounces) Italian turkey sausage links
- 2 teaspoons grated lemon peel
- ⅓ cup lemon juice
- ⅓ cup olive oil
- 2 tablespoons minced fresh basil
- 2 teaspoons Italian seasoning
- 3 garlic cloves, minced
- 1 jar (12 ounces) roasted sweet red peppers, drained and thinly sliced
- 1 cup pitted Greek olives
- 1 pound fresh mozzarella cheese, cut into ½-inch cubes

1. Cook sausages according to package directions; cool slightly. Meanwhile, whisk together lemon peel, lemon juice, oil, basil, Italian seasoning and garlic.
2. Slice the sausages and place in a large bowl; add peppers and olives. Toss with dressing. Refrigerate, covered, overnight.
3. Remove the sausage mixture from refrigerator; stir in cheese. Let stand 30 minutes before serving.

SWISS & CARAWAY FLATBREADS

My mom came across this rustic-looking flatbread recipe many years ago and always made it on Christmas Eve. Now I make it for my own family throughout the year. It's easy to double or cut in half depending on how many you're serving.
—**DIANE BERGER** SEQUIM, WA

PREP: 20 MIN. + RISING • **BAKE:** 10 MIN.
MAKES: 2 LOAVES (16 PIECES EACH)

- 2 loaves (1 pound each) frozen bread dough, thawed
- ¼ cup butter, melted
- ¼ cup canola oil
- 1 tablespoon dried minced onion
- 1 tablespoon Dijon mustard
- 2 teaspoons caraway seeds
- 1 teaspoon Worcestershire sauce
- 1 tablespoon dry sherry, optional
- 2 cups shredded Swiss cheese

1. On a lightly floured surface, roll each portion of dough into a 15x10-in. rectangle. Transfer to two greased 15x10x1-in. baking pans. Cover with kitchen towels; let rise in a warm place until doubled, about 45 minutes.
2. Preheat the oven to 425°. Using fingertips, press several dimples into dough. In a small bowl, whisk melted butter, oil, onion, mustard, caraway seeds, Worcestershire sauce and, if desired, sherry until blended; brush over dough. Sprinkle with cheese. Bake 10-15 minutes or until golden brown. Serve warm.
FREEZE OPTION *Let the flatbreads cool, then cut them into pieces. Freeze in resealable plastic freezer bags. To use, reheat flatbreads on an ungreased baking sheet in a preheated 425° oven until heated through.*

SWISS & CARAWAY FLATBREADS

MUSHROOM BUNDLES

I love creating my own party starters. When I made these crispy bundles for New Year's Eve, they were gone in a flash.
—**TINA COOPMAN** TORONTO, ON

PREP: 30 MIN. • **BAKE:** 15 MIN.
MAKES: 1 DOZEN

- 1 tablespoon olive oil
- 1 cup chopped fresh mushrooms
- 1 cup chopped baby portobello mushrooms
- ¼ cup finely chopped red onion
- 2 garlic cloves, minced
- ¼ teaspoon dried rosemary, crushed
- ⅛ teaspoon pepper
- 4 sheets phyllo dough (14x9-inch size)
- 3 tablespoons butter, melted
- 2 tablespoons crumbled feta cheese

1. Preheat oven to 375°. In a large skillet, heat oil over medium-high heat. Add mushrooms and onion; cook and stir 4-5 minutes or until tender. Add garlic, rosemary and pepper; cook 2 minutes longer. Remove from heat.

2. Place one sheet of phyllo dough on a work surface; brush with butter. (Keep remaining phyllo covered with plastic wrap and a damp towel to prevent it from drying out.) Layer with three additional phyllo sheets, brushing each layer. Using a sharp knife, cut the layered sheets into twelve 3-in. squares. Carefully press each stack into an ungreased mini-muffin cup.

3. Stir feta into mushroom mixture; spoon 1 tablespoon into each phyllo cup. Form into bundles by gathering edges of phyllo squares and twisting centers to close. Brush tops with remaining butter. Bake 12-15 minutes or until golden brown. Serve warm.

FREEZE OPTION *Freeze cooled pastries in resealable plastic freezer bags. To use, reheat pastries on a greased baking sheet in a preheated 375° oven until they are crisp and heated through.*

ALMOND CHEDDAR APPETIZERS

I always try to have a supply of these appetizers on-hand in the freezer. If guests drop in, I just pull some out and bake to serve. They work great as a snack, for brunch or along with a lighter lunch.
—**LINDA THOMPSON** SOUTHAMPTON, ON

START TO FINISH: 25 MIN.
MAKES: ABOUT 4 DOZEN

- 1 cup mayonnaise
- 2 teaspoons Worcestershire sauce
- 1 cup shredded sharp cheddar cheese
- 1 medium onion, chopped
- ¾ cup slivered almonds, chopped
- 6 bacon strips, cooked and crumbled
- 1 loaf (1 pound) French bread

1. In a bowl, combine the mayonnaise and Worcestershire sauce; stir in cheese, onion, almonds and bacon.
2. Cut bread into ½-in. slices; spread with cheese mixture. Cut slices in half; place on a greased baking sheet. Bake at 400° for 8-10 minutes or until the topping is bubbly.

FREEZE OPTION *Place unbaked appetizers in a single layer on a baking sheet; freeze for 1 hour. Remove from the baking sheet and store in an airtight container for up to 2 months. When ready to use, place unthawed appetizers on a greased baking sheet. Bake at 400° for 10 minutes or until topping is bubbly.*

MUSHROOM BUNDLES

✱
DID YOU KNOW? You can refrigerate unopened phyllo dough for up to 3 weeks or freeze it for up to 3 months. Opened dough can be refrigerated for up to 3 days. Baked phyllo products can be stored in an airtight container for up to 3 days or frozen.

ALMOND CHEDDAR
APPETIZERS

SALSA VERDE

The tomatillos I grew last year were so abundant that I had enough to eat fresh and some to freeze for future gatherings. I like to add extra zip by juicing a fresh lime into the salsa.

—**KIM BANICK** SALEM, OR

PREP: 15 MIN. • **BAKE:** 35 MIN.
MAKES: 2 CUPS

- 2 **pounds medium tomatillos (about 16), husks removed and halved**
- 2 **large sweet onions, coarsely chopped (about 4 cups)**
- 2 **serrano peppers, seeded and chopped**
- 6 **garlic cloves, peeled and halved**
- ¼ **cup olive oil**
- ⅓ **to ½ cup water**
- ½ **cup chopped fresh cilantro**
- 2 **tablespoons lime juice**
- 1 **teaspoon salt**

1. Preheat oven to 425°. In a large bowl, toss tomatillos, onions, peppers and garlic with oil. Divide the mixture between two 15x10x1-in. baking pans. Roast for 35-40 minutes or until lightly browned, stirring occasionally. Cool slightly.
2. Process the tomatillo mixture in a food processor until smooth, adding water to reach desired consistency. Add the remaining ingredients; pulse just until combined.
FREEZE OPTION *Freeze the cooled salsa in freezer containers. To use, thaw completely in refrigerator.*
NOTE *Wear disposable gloves when cutting hot peppers; the oils can burn skin. Avoid touching your face.*

SALSA VERDE

MOROCCAN EMPANADAS

MOROCCAN EMPANADAS

My family goes for Moroccan flavors, so I make these flaky beef hand pies with apricot preserves in both the filling and the spicy dipping sauce.

—**ARLENE ERLBACH** MORTON GROVE, IL

PREP: 30 MIN. • **BAKE:** 15 MIN.
MAKES: 20 SERVINGS

- ¾ **pound ground beef**
- 1 **medium onion, chopped**
- 3 **ounces cream cheese, softened**
- ⅓ **cup apricot preserves**
- ¼ **cup finely chopped carrot**
- ¾ **teaspoon Moroccan seasoning (ras el hanout) or ½ teaspoon ground cumin plus ¼ teaspoon ground coriander and dash cayenne pepper**
- ¼ **teaspoon salt**
- 3 **sheets refrigerated pie pastry**
- 1 **large egg yolk, beaten**
- 1 **tablespoon sesame seeds**

SAUCE
- ½ **cup apricot preserves**
- ½ **cup chili sauce**

1. Preheat oven to 425°. In a large skillet, cook beef and onion over medium heat for 5-7 minutes or until beef is no longer pink, breaking up beef into crumbles; drain. Stir in cream cheese, preserves, carrot and seasonings. Cool slightly.
2. On a lightly floured work surface, unroll pastry. Cut out 40 circles with a floured 3-in. cookie cutter; reroll the dough as necessary. Place half of the circles 2 in. apart on parchment paper-lined baking sheets. Top each with 1 rounded tablespoon of the beef mixture. Top each with a second pastry circle; press the edges with a fork to seal.
3. Brush tops with egg yolk; sprinkle with sesame seeds. Cut slits in tops. Bake 12-15 minutes or until golden brown. Remove from pan to a wire rack to cool.
4. Meanwhile, in a microwave, warm the sauce ingredients, stirring to combine. Serve with empanadas.
FREEZE OPTION *Cover and freeze unbaked empanadas on waxed paper-lined baking sheets until firm. Transfer to resealable plastic freezer bags; return to freezer. To use, bake empanadas as directed, increasing time as necessary. Prepare sauce as directed.*

MUSHROOM PALMIERS

I found this recipe a long time ago when I worked at a museum in West Texas and attended a fundraiser where it was served. Years later, it's still a huge hit at parties! Frozen puff pastry helps make it easy. The palmiers freeze well too.
—JUDY LOCK PANHANDLE, TX

PREP: 20 MIN. + COOLING
BAKE: 15 MIN./BATCH
MAKES: 4 DOZEN

- 2 tablespoons butter
- ¾ pound fresh mushrooms, finely chopped
- 1 small onion, finely chopped
- 1 teaspoon minced fresh thyme or ¼ teaspoon dried thyme
- ¾ teaspoon lemon juice
- ¾ teaspoon hot pepper sauce
- ¼ teaspoon salt
- 1 package (17.3 ounces) frozen puff pastry, thawed
- 1 large egg
- 2 teaspoons water

1. Preheat oven to 400°. In a large skillet, heat butter over medium heat. Add mushrooms and onion; cook and stir until tender. Stir in thyme, lemon juice, hot pepper sauce and salt. Cool mixture completely.

2. Unfold one pastry sheet. Spread half of the mushroom mixture to within ½ in. of edges. Roll the left and right sides toward the center, jelly-roll style, until the rolls meet in the middle. Cut into 24 slices. Repeat with the remaining pastry and mushrooms.

3. Place on greased baking sheets. In a small bowl, whisk egg and water; brush over pastries. Bake for 15-20 minutes or until golden brown. Serve warm or at room temperature.

FREEZE OPTION *Freeze cooled appetizers in freezer containers, separating layers with waxed paper. To use, preheat oven to 400°. Reheat appetizers on a greased baking sheet until crisp and heated through.*

MARMALADE MEATBALLS

⑤INGREDIENTS SLOW COOKER

MARMALADE MEATBALLS

I brought this snappy recipe to work for a potluck. I started cooking the meatballs in the morning, and by lunchtime they were ready. They disappeared fast!
—JEANNE KISS GREENSBURG, PA

PREP: 10 MIN. • **COOK:** 4 HOURS
MAKES: ABOUT 5 DOZEN

- 1 bottle (16 ounces) Catalina salad dressing
- 1 cup orange marmalade
- 3 tablespoons Worcestershire sauce
- ½ teaspoon crushed red pepper flakes
- 1 package (32 ounces) frozen fully cooked home-style meatballs, thawed

In a 3-qt. slow cooker, combine the salad dressing, marmalade, Worcestershire sauce and pepper flakes. Stir in meatballs. Cover and cook on low for 4-5 hours or until heated through.

FREEZE OPTION *Freeze cooled meatball mixture in freezer containers. To use, partially thaw in refrigerator overnight. Microwave, covered, on high in a microwave-safe dish until heated through, gently stirring and adding a little water if necessary.*

EASY PARTY MEATBALLS *Omit first four ingredients. Combine 1 bottle (14 ounces) ketchup, ¼ cup A.1. steak sauce, 1 tablespoon minced garlic and 1 teaspoon Dijon mustard in slow cooker; stir in meatballs. Cook as directed for Marmalade Meatballs.*

MUSHROOM PALMIERS

CRISPY BAKED WONTONS

ONION BRIE BOWL

Golden caramelized onions are paired with buttery, silky Brie in this warm spread. Make sure to have enough bread cubes or crackers on hand to scoop up every gooey bit!
—*TASTE OF HOME* TEST KITCHEN

PREP: 40 MIN. • **BAKE:** 25 MIN. + STANDING
MAKES: 18 SERVINGS

- 3 **cups sliced onions**
- 2 **tablespoons canola oil**
- 1 **tablespoon brown sugar**
- 1 **tablespoon balsamic vinegar**
- ½ **teaspoon salt**
- 1 **round loaf sourdough bread (1 pound)**
- 1 **round (8 ounces) Brie cheese**

1. In a large skillet, saute onions in oil until softened. Reduce the heat to medium-low; add the brown sugar, vinegar and salt. Cook, stirring occasionally, for 30-35 minutes or until onions are deep golden brown.
2. Cut top third off loaf of bread; hollow out enough bread from the bottom to make room for cheese. Cube the removed bread; set aside. Using a knife, make 2-in. cuts into the loaf around the edge at 1-in. intervals. Remove rind from cheese; cut cheese in half horizontally. Layer half of the cheese and onions in the loaf. Repeat the layers.
3. Transfer to an ungreased baking sheet. Bake at 350° for 25-30 minutes or until the cheese is melted. Let stand for 10 minutes. Serve brie bowl with the bread cubes.

FREEZE OPTION *Cool onion mixture. Assemble loaf, cheese and onion mixture as directed, then wrap and freeze; freeze bread cubes in a separate freezer container. To use, partially thaw in refrigerator overnight. Remove from refrigerator 30 minutes before baking. Bake the bread bowl as directed, increasing the time as necessary until heated through. Serve with bread cubes.*

CRISPY BAKED WONTONS

These quick, versatile wontons are great for a savory snack or paired with a bowl of soothing soup on a cold day. I usually make a large batch and freeze half.
—**BRIANNA SHADE** BEAVERTON, OR

PREP: 30 MIN. • **BAKE:** 10 MIN.
MAKES: ABOUT 4 DOZEN

- ½ **pound ground pork**
- ½ **pound extra-lean ground turkey**
- 1 **small onion, chopped**
- 1 **can (8 ounces) sliced water chestnuts, drained and chopped**
- ⅓ **cup reduced-sodium soy sauce**
- ¼ **cup egg substitute**
- 1½ **teaspoons ground ginger**
- 1 **package (12 ounces) wonton wrappers**
  Cooking spray
  Sweet-and-sour sauce, optional

1. In a large skillet, cook the pork, turkey and onion over medium heat until meat is no longer pink; drain. Transfer to a large bowl. Stir in the water chestnuts, soy sauce, egg substitute and ginger.
2. Position a wonton wrapper with one point toward you. (Keep the remaining wrappers covered with a damp paper towel until ready to use.) Place 2 heaping teaspoons of filling in the center of the wrapper. Fold bottom corner over filling; fold sides toward center over filling. Roll toward the remaining point. Moisten top corner with water; press to seal. Repeat with the remaining wrappers and filling.
3. Place on baking sheets coated with cooking spray; lightly coat wontons with additional cooking spray.
4. Bake at 400° for 10-12 minutes or until golden brown, turning once. Serve warm, with sweet-and-sour sauce if desired.

FREEZE OPTION *Freeze cooled baked wontons in a freezer container, separating layers with waxed paper. To use, reheat on a baking sheet in a preheated 400° oven until wontons are crisp and heated through.*

APPLE-NUT BLUE CHEESE TARTLETS

These tasty appetizers look and taste gourmet, but they're easy to make and have loads of blue cheese flavor. The phyllo shells and filling can be made in advance: just fill the cups and warm them in the oven before serving. Garnish with fresh parsley or other herbs if you like.

—**TRISHA KRUSE** EAGLE, ID

PREP: 25 MIN. • **BAKE:** 10 MIN.
MAKES: 15 APPETIZERS

- 1 **large apple, peeled and finely chopped**
- 1 **medium onion, finely chopped**
- 2 **teaspoons butter**
- 1 **cup crumbled blue cheese**
- 4 **tablespoons finely chopped walnuts, toasted, divided**
- ½ **teaspoon salt**
- 1 **package (1.9 ounces) frozen miniature phyllo tart shells**

1. In a small nonstick skillet, saute apple and onion in butter until tender. Remove from the heat; stir in blue cheese, 3 tablespoons walnuts and salt. Spoon a rounded tablespoonful into each tart shell.
2. Place on an ungreased baking sheet. Bake at 350° for 5 minutes. Sprinkle with remaining walnuts; bake 2-3 minutes longer or until lightly browned.

FREEZE OPTION *Freeze cooled pastries in a freezer container, separating layers with waxed paper. To use, reheat pastries on a baking sheet in a preheated 350° oven until crisp and heated through.*

✳

DID YOU KNOW? "Blue" cheese is a general classification of veined cheese; feel free to experiment by using Roquefort, Gorgonzola, Stilton, or the blue-, green-, or blue-gray veined cheese of your choice!

APPLE-NUT BLUE CHEESE TARTLETS

SOUPS, SIDES & MORE

Homemade soup is the best kind of comfort food.
Here are some soups that you can have waiting
for you when you get home in the evening, soups
that freeze well so you'll always have them
on hand, and some delicious side dishes, too!

SUMMER SQUASH & WHITE BEAN SOUP, P. 22

SUMMER SQUASH & WHITE BEAN SOUP

I love using summer squash in soups. This one's hearty as is, but stir in chopped ham for an extra wallop of flavor. Serve this warm or chilled.

—**SARA HORNBECK** KNOXVILLE, TN

START TO FINISH: 30 MIN.
MAKES: 6 SERVINGS (2¼ QUARTS)

- 2 **tablespoons butter**
- 2 **tablespoons olive oil**
- 2 **large sweet onions, chopped (about 4 cups)**
- 2 **garlic cloves, minced**
- 4 **medium yellow summer squash, cubed (about 6 cups)**
- 1 **carton (32 ounces) chicken broth**
- 2 **cans (15 ounces each) white kidney or cannellini beans, rinsed and drained, divided**
- ¼ **cup minced fresh parsley**
- 1 **to 2 tablespoons minced fresh tarragon**
- ¾ **teaspoon salt**
- ¾ **cup plain Greek yogurt**

1. In a 6-qt. stockpot, heat butter and oil over medium heat. Add onions; cook and stir 6-8 minutes or until tender. Add garlic; cook 1 minute longer.
2. Add the squash and broth; bring to a boil. Reduce heat; simmer, uncovered, 10-12 minutes or until the squash is tender. Stir in one can of beans, parsley, tarragon and salt. Puree soup using an immersion blender. Or, cool soup slightly and puree in batches in a blender. Return to pan; stir in the remaining can of beans and heat through. Top each serving with a spoonful of yogurt.
FREEZE OPTION *Freeze cooled soup in freezer containers. To use, partially thaw in refrigerator overnight. Heat through in a saucepan, stirring occasionally and adding a little broth if necessary.*

✳

DID YOU KNOW? Vegetable broth is an easy swap for chicken broth—but not all vegetable broths are vegetarian. Read the label or contact the manufacturer to make sure no chicken was added to the broth during processing.

MARINATED CARROTS

BARLEY CORN SALAD

A great alternative to pasta salads, this fresh, fast dish adds summery flavor to barley and sweet corn. Take it to your next get-together and see how fast it disappears!

—MARY ANN KIEFFER LAWRENCE, KS

PREP: 15 MIN. + CHILLING
MAKES: 6 SERVINGS

- 2 cups cooked medium pearl barley
- 2 cups frozen corn, thawed
- ½ cup chopped sweet red pepper
- ½ cup chopped green pepper
- 3 green onions, chopped
- 1 tablespoon minced fresh cilantro
- 2 tablespoons lemon juice
- 2 tablespoons canola oil
- ½ teaspoon salt
- ½ teaspoon dried thyme
- ⅛ teaspoon pepper

In a large bowl, combine the first six ingredients. In a jar with a tight-fitting lid, combine the lemon juice, oil, salt, thyme and pepper; shake well. Drizzle over the salad and toss to coat. Cover and refrigerate for at least 2 hours before serving.

FREEZE OPTION *Prepare salad without onions and cilantro. Transfer to freezer containers; freeze. To use, thaw completely in refrigerator. Gently stir in onions, cilantro and a little oil if necessary.*

TEST KITCHEN TIP *Cook a large batch of barley and keep it in the freezer in 1-cup amounts ready for use in salads, soups or stews.*

MARINATED CARROTS

Carrots take a step up in flavor with this simple, tangy-sweet marinade. Put this dish in the fridge the night before and take it out when you're ready to serve!

—SHANNON EMMANUEL CHARLOTTE, NC

PREP: 20 MIN. + MARINATING
MAKES: 2 SERVINGS

- ½ pound fresh baby carrots
- ¼ cup chopped onion
- ¼ cup chopped green pepper
- ½ cup tomato sauce
- 2 tablespoons sugar
- 2 tablespoons cider vinegar
- 1 tablespoon vegetable oil
- ½ teaspoon Worcestershire sauce
- ¼ teaspoon salt
- ¼ teaspoon pepper

1. Place 1 in. of water in a small saucepan; add carrots. Bring to a boil. Reduce heat; cover and simmer for 8-10 minutes or until crisp-tender. Drain.
2. In a small bowl, combine carrots, onion and green pepper. In another bowl, combine the tomato sauce, sugar, vinegar, oil, Worcestershire sauce, salt and pepper. Pour over carrot mixture and stir to coat. Cover and refrigerate for several hours or overnight. Serve with a slotted spoon.

BARLEY CORN SALAD

PICO DE GALLO BLACK BEAN SOUP

Everyone at my table goes for this feel-good soup. It's quick when you're pressed for time and beats fast food hands down.

—DARLIS WILFER WEST BEND, WI

START TO FINISH: 20 MIN.
MAKES: 6 SERVINGS

- 4 cans (15 ounces each) black beans, rinsed and drained
- 2 cups vegetable broth
- 2 cups pico de gallo
- ½ cup water
- 2 teaspoons ground cumin
  Chopped fresh cilantro
  Additional pico de gallo, optional

1. In a Dutch oven, combine the first five ingredients; bring to a boil over medium heat, stirring occasionally. Reduce heat; simmer, uncovered, 5-7 minutes or until the vegetables in the pico de gallo are softened, stirring occasionally.

2. Puree soup using an immersion blender. Or, cool soup slightly and puree in batches in a blender; return to pan and heat through. Serve with chopped cilantro and more pico de gallo as desired.

FREEZE OPTION *Freeze cooled soup in freezer containers. To use, partially thaw in the refrigerator overnight. Heat through in a saucepan, stirring occasionally and adding a little broth or water if necessary. Top as desired.*

CHIPOTLE BEEF CHILI

PICO DE GALLO BLACK BEAN SOUP

SLOW COOKER 🍲
CHIPOTLE BEEF CHILI

I love spicy food, so this chili really hits the spot. If you are sensitive to chili peppers, start out with one or two chipotles and add more until you hit your spice limit!

—STEVEN SCHEND GRAND RAPIDS, MI

PREP: 15 MIN. • **COOK:** 6 HOURS
MAKES: 8 SERVINGS (ABOUT 2½ QUARTS)

- 2 pounds beef flank steak, cut into 1-inch pieces
- 2 to 4 chipotle peppers in adobo sauce, chopped
- ¼ cup chopped onion
- 1 tablespoon chili powder
- 2 garlic cloves, minced
- 1 teaspoon salt
- ½ teaspoon ground cumin
- 3 cans (15 ounces each) tomato puree
- 1 can (14½ ounces) beef broth
- ¼ cup minced fresh cilantro
  Sour cream, optional

In a 4- or 5-qt. slow cooker, combine first nine ingredients. Cook, covered, on low for 6-8 hours or until the meat is tender. Stir in cilantro; top with sour cream if desired.

FREEZE OPTION *Freeze cooled chili in freezer containers. To use, partially thaw in the refrigerator overnight. Heat through in a saucepan, stirring occasionally and adding a little broth or water if necessary.*

GREEK HERB RATATOUILLE

When I lived in Florida, I went to a dinner at a friend's home. His wife, who is Greek, served a beautiful side dish she called an eggplant fan. While I've made her version many times with great success, I was inspired by the movie *Ratatouille* to create this version.

—JOE SHERWOOD TRYON, NE

PREP: 30 MIN. + CHILLING • **BAKE:** 45 MIN.
MAKES: 13 SERVINGS (¾ CUP EACH)

- 1 small eggplant
- 2 small zucchini
- 2 small yellow summer squash
- 4 plum tomatoes
- 1 large sweet onion
- ½ cup butter, melted
- ½ cup minced fresh parsley
- 3 garlic cloves, minced
- ½ teaspoon salt
- ½ teaspoon each dried thyme, oregano, tarragon and basil
- ½ teaspoon dried rosemary, crushed
- ½ teaspoon pepper
- 1 cup shredded part-skim mozzarella cheese

1. Cut vegetables into ¼-in. thick slices.
2. In a greased 13x9-in. baking dish, layer the eggplant, zucchini, squash, tomatoes and onion. In a small bowl, combine butter, parsley, garlic and seasonings; pour over the vegetables. Cover and refrigerate overnight.
3. Remove from the refrigerator 30 minutes before baking. Bake, uncovered, at 375° for 35 minutes. Sprinkle with cheese. Bake for 10-15 minutes longer or until the cheese is melted. Serve with a slotted spoon.

BIG-BATCH DINNER ROLLS

Homemade rolls are always in demand, so I make them ahead, partially bake and freeze. They zoom from freezer to oven when guests are on the way.

—MARY JANE HENDERSON SALEM, NJ

PREP: 25 MIN. + RISING • **BAKE:** 15 MIN.
MAKES: 4 DOZEN

- 2 packages (¼ ounce each) active dry yeast
- 1 cup warm water (110° to 115°)
- 2 cups warm 2% milk (110° to 115°)
- ½ cup shortening
- ¼ cup sugar
- 3 teaspoons salt
- 10 cups all-purpose flour

1. In a small bowl, dissolve yeast in warm water. In a large bowl, combine milk, shortening, sugar, salt, yeast mixture and 2½ cups flour; beat on medium speed until smooth. Stir in enough of the remaining flour to form a stiff dough.
2. Turn the dough onto a floured surface; knead until smooth and elastic, about 6-8 minutes. Place in a greased bowl, turning once to grease the top. Cover with plastic wrap and let rise in a warm place until doubled, about 1½ hours.
3. Punch down dough. Turn onto a lightly floured surface; divide and shape into 48 balls. Place 2 in. apart on greased baking sheets. Cover with kitchen towels; let rise in a warm place until doubled, about 20 minutes.
4. Preheat oven to 375°. Bake for 12-15 minutes or until golden brown.
FREEZE OPTION *Partially bake rolls at 325° for 10 minutes. Freeze cooled, partially baked rolls in resealable plastic freezer bags. To use, bake frozen rolls on greased baking sheets at 375° for 12-15 minutes or until golden brown.*

GREEK HERB RATATOUILLE

DIJON VEGGIES WITH COUSCOUS

ONION FRENCH LOAVES

I regularly bake French bread to serve with soup. I love variety, so I created these tasty loaves by adding dried minced onion to my usual recipe in an attempt to capture another bread that I had tasted.

—RUTH FUELLER BARMSTEDT, GERMANY

PREP: 25 MIN. + RISING • **BAKE:** 20 MIN.
MAKES: 2 LOAVES (¾ POUND AND 16 SLICES EACH)

- 1 cup water (70° to 80°)
- ½ cup dried minced onion
- 1 tablespoon sugar
- 2 teaspoons salt
- 3 cups bread flour
- 2¼ teaspoons active dry yeast
- 1 tablespoon cornmeal
- 1 large egg yolk, lightly beaten

1. In bread machine pan, place the first six ingredients in order suggested by manufacturer. Select dough setting (check after 5 minutes of mixing; add 1 to 2 tablespoons of water or flour if needed).
2. When cycle is completed, turn dough onto a lightly floured surface. Cover and let rest for 15 minutes. Divide dough in half. Roll each portion into a 15x10-in. rectangle. Roll up jelly-roll style, starting with a long side; pinch seams to seal. Pinch ends to seal and tuck under.
3. Sprinkle cornmeal onto a greased baking sheet. Place loaves on pan. Cover and let rise in a warm place until doubled, about 30 minutes. Brush with egg yolk. Make ¼-in.-deep cuts 2 in. apart in each loaf.
4. Bake at 375° for 20-25 minutes or until golden brown. Remove from pan to a wire rack.

FREEZE OPTION *Securely wrap and freeze cooled loaves in heavy-duty foil. To use, place a foil-wrapped loaf on a baking sheet and reheat in a 450° oven for 10-15 minutes. Carefully remove hot foil; return to oven for a few minutes to crisp the crust.*

✳

TEST KITCHEN TIP If dough doesn't rise in your bread machine, try rinsing the container with hot tap water before starting. A cold container will lower the temperature of your warm water.

DIJON VEGGIES WITH COUSCOUS

Coated in a tangy Dijon sauce, these tasty veggies and fluffy couscous make for a delightful side.

—JULIANA DUMITRU FAIRVIEW PARK, OH

PREP: 20 MIN. • **BAKE:** 20 MIN.
MAKES: 6 SERVINGS

- ½ pound medium fresh mushrooms, quartered
- 1 medium zucchini, halved lengthwise and cut into ¼-inch slices
- 1 medium sweet red pepper, cut into 1-inch pieces
- ¼ cup dry red wine or reduced-sodium chicken broth
- 3 tablespoons Dijon mustard
- 2 tablespoons olive oil
- 2 garlic cloves, minced
- 1 teaspoon prepared horseradish
- ½ teaspoon salt
- ¼ teaspoon pepper
- 1 cup water
- 1 cup uncooked couscous

1. Place an 18x12-in. piece of heavy-duty foil on a baking sheet; set aside.
2. In a large bowl, combine the mushrooms, zucchini and red pepper. Combine wine, mustard, oil, garlic, horseradish, salt and pepper; drizzle over vegetables. Toss to coat; transfer to baking sheet. Top with a second large piece of foil. Bring edges of foil pieces together; crimp to seal, forming a large packet.
3. Bake at 350° for 20-25 minutes or until vegetables are tender. Open foil carefully to allow steam to escape.
4. In a small saucepan, bring water to a boil. Stir in couscous. Remove from the heat; cover , let stand 5-10 minutes or until water is absorbed. Fluff with fork. Transfer couscous, vegetables to a large serving bowl; toss to combine.

FREEZE OPTION *Freeze cooled couscous mixture in a freezer container. To use, partially thaw in refrigerator overnight. Microwave, covered, on high in a microwave-safe dish until heated through, adding 2-3 tablespoons water to moisten.*

RUSTIC ITALIAN TORTELLINI SOUP

This soup is quick to fix on a busy night and full of healthy, tasty ingredients. The original recipe called for spicy sausage links, but turkey sausage or even ground turkey breast is just as good. For variety, try swapping ravioli for the tortellini.

—TRACY FASNACHT IRWIN, PA

PREP: 20 MIN. • **COOK:** 20 MIN.
MAKES: 6 SERVINGS (2 QUARTS)

- ¾ pound Italian turkey sausage links, casings removed
- 1 medium onion, chopped
- 6 garlic cloves, minced
- 2 cans (14½ ounces each) reduced-sodium chicken broth
- 1¾ cups water
- 1 can (14½ ounces) diced tomatoes, undrained
- 1 package (9 ounces) refrigerated cheese tortellini
- 1 package (6 ounces) fresh baby spinach, coarsely chopped
- 2¼ teaspoons minced fresh basil or ¾ teaspoon dried basil
- ¼ teaspoon pepper
  Dash crushed red pepper flakes
  Shredded Parmesan cheese, optional

1. Crumble sausage into a Dutch oven; add onion. Cook and stir over medium heat until the meat is no longer pink. Add garlic; cook 1 minute longer. Stir in the broth, water and tomatoes. Bring to a boil.

2. Add tortellini; return to a boil. Cook for 5-8 minutes or until almost tender, stirring occasionally. Reduce heat; add spinach, basil, pepper and pepper flakes. Cook 2-3 minutes longer or until the spinach is wilted and the tortellini are tender. Serve with cheese if desired.

FREEZE OPTION *Place individual portions of cooled soup in freezer containers and freeze. To use, partially thaw in refrigerator overnight. Heat through in a saucepan, stirring occasionally and adding a little broth if necessary.*

DELUXE HASH BROWN CASSEROLE

My son-in-law gave me the recipe for this hash brown casserole, which my kids say is addictive. It's also an amazing make-ahead dish.

—AMY OSWALT BURR, NE

PREP: 10 MIN. • **BAKE:** 50 MIN. + COOLING
MAKES: 12 SERVINGS (⅔ CUP EACH)

- 1½ cups sour cream onion dip
- 1 can (10¾ ounces) condensed cream of chicken soup, undiluted
- 1 envelope ranch salad dressing mix
- 1 teaspoon onion powder
- 1 teaspoon garlic powder
- ½ teaspoon pepper
- 1 package (30 ounces) frozen shredded hash brown potatoes, thawed
- 2 cups shredded cheddar cheese
- ½ cup crumbled cooked bacon

Preheat oven to 375°. In a large bowl, mix the first six ingredients; stir in potatoes, cheese and bacon. Transfer to a greased 13x9-in. baking dish. Bake 50-60 minutes or until golden brown.

FREEZE OPTION *Cover and freeze unbaked casserole. To use, partially thaw in refrigerator overnight. Remove from refrigerator 30 minutes before baking. Preheat oven to 375°. Bake casserole as directed, increasing time to 1¼ to 1½ hours or until top is golden brown and a thermometer inserted in center reads 165°.*

DELUXE HASH BROWN CASSEROLE

PECAN RICE PILAF

This is one of my stand-by side dishes, which can complement most meat and meatless entrees. It is special enough for company yet quick enough for busy weeknights.

—JACQUELINE OGLESBY SPRUCE PINE, NC

PREP: 15 MIN. • **COOK:** 20 MIN.
MAKES: 9 SERVINGS

- 1 cup chopped pecans
- 5 tablespoons butter, divided
- 1 small onion, chopped
- 2 cups uncooked long grain rice
- 1 carton (32 ounces) chicken broth
- 3 tablespoons minced fresh parsley, divided
- ½ teaspoon salt
- ¼ teaspoon dried thyme
- ⅛ teaspoon pepper
- 1 cup shredded carrots

1. In a large saucepan, saute pecans in 2 tablespoons butter until toasted; remove from the pan and set aside.
2. In the same pan, saute onion in the remaining butter until tender. Add rice; cook and stir for 3-4 minutes or until the rice is lightly browned. Stir in broth, 2 tablespoons parsley, salt, thyme and pepper. Bring to a boil. Reduce heat; cover and simmer for 10 minutes.
3. Add carrots; simmer 3-5 minutes longer or until the rice is tender. Stir in toasted pecans and remaining parsley. Fluff with a fork.
FREEZE OPTION *Reserving pecans for later, freeze cooled pilaf in a freezer container. To use, partially thaw in refrigerator overnight. Microwave, covered, on high in a microwave-safe dish until heated through, adding 2-3 tablespoons water to moisten. Toast pecans; add to pilaf.*

ROSEMARY FLATBREADS

My family likes this bread recipe as a pizza crust. But with touches of olive oil and fresh herbs, it becomes a lovely flatbread side dish or savory appetizer.

—SUE BROWN WEST BEND, WI

PREP: 40 MIN. + RISING • **BAKE:** 10 MIN.
MAKES: 6 SERVINGS

- 1 package (¼ ounce) active dry yeast
- ¼ cup plus ⅓ cup warm water (110° to 115°), divided
- ½ teaspoon honey
- 2 cups all-purpose flour, divided
- 1 tablespoon olive oil
- 1 teaspoon minced fresh rosemary
- ½ teaspoon kosher salt

TOPPING
- 1 tablespoon olive oil
- 1 teaspoon minced fresh rosemary
- ½ teaspoon kosher salt

1. In a small bowl, dissolve yeast in ¼ cup warm water; stir in honey. Add ¼ cup flour; mix until almost smooth. Let stand 30 minutes or until bubbly.
2. Place remaining flour, remaining warm water, oil, rosemary and salt in a food processor; add the yeast mixture. Process until dough forms a ball. Process 1 minute more to knead the dough, pulsing as needed.
3. Transfer to a greased bowl, turning once to grease the top. Cover with plastic wrap and let rise in a warm place until doubled, about 1 hour.
4. Punch down dough. Turn onto a lightly floured surface; divide and shape dough into six balls. On greased baking sheets, pat each ball into a 5-in. circle. For topping, brush tops with oil; sprinkle with rosemary and salt. Bake 8-12 minutes or until golden brown. Serve warm.
FREEZE OPTION *Freeze cooled flatbreads in a resealable plastic freezer bag. To use, thaw at room temperature or, if desired, microwave each flatbread on high 10-15 seconds or until heated through.*

PECAN RICE PILAF

SLOW COOKER TURKEY CHILI

FREEZE OPTION *Freeze cooled chili in freezer containers. To use, partially thaw in refrigerator overnight. Heat through in saucepan, stirring occasionally and adding broth or water if necessary.*

⑤INGREDIENTS

SPICY PUMPKIN & CORN SOUP

A seriously quick dish, this soup can satisfy a hungry household in 20 minutes. My family loves this soup served with a hot pan of corn bread.

—**HEATHER ROREX** WINNEMUCCA, NV

START TO FINISH: 20 MIN.
MAKES: 8 SERVINGS

- 1 **can (15 ounces) solid-pack pumpkin**
- 1 **can (15 ounces) black beans, rinsed and drained**
- 1½ **cups frozen corn**
- 1 **can (10 ounces) diced tomatoes and green chilies**
- 2 **cans (14½ ounces each) reduced-sodium chicken broth**
- ¼ **teaspoon pepper**

In a large saucepan, mix all ingredients. Bring to a boil. Reduce heat; simmer, uncovered, for 10-15 minutes or until slightly thickened, stirring occasionally.

FREEZE OPTION *Freeze cooled soup in freezer containers. To use, partially thaw in refrigerator overnight. Heat through in a saucepan, stirring occasionally and adding a little broth if necessary.*

SLOW COOKER 🍲

SLOW COOKER TURKEY CHILI

I love this recipe because I can prepare it in the morning, and a delicious, wholesome dinner is ready when I get home in the evening. And you can make a big batch to freeze!

—**TERRI CRANDALL** GARDNERVILLE, NV

PREP: 30 MIN. • **COOK:** 7¼ HOURS
MAKES: 8 SERVINGS (2¾ QUARTS)

- 2 **tablespoons olive oil**
- 1½ **pounds ground turkey**
- 1 **medium onion, chopped**
- 2 **tablespoons ground ancho chili pepper**
- 1 **tablespoon chili powder**
- 1½ **teaspoons salt**
- 1½ **teaspoons ground cumin**
- 1½ **teaspoons paprika**
- 2 **cans (14½ ounces each) fire-roasted diced tomatoes, undrained**
- 1 **medium sweet yellow pepper, chopped**
- 1 **medium sweet red pepper, chopped**
- 1 **can (4 ounces) chopped green chilies**
- 1 **garlic clove, minced**
- 1 **cup brewed coffee**
- ¾ **cup dry red wine or chicken broth**
- 1 **can (16 ounces) kidney beans, rinsed and drained**
- 1 **can (15 ounces) white kidney or cannellini beans, rinsed and drained**
  Sliced avocado and chopped green onions

1. In a skillet over medium heat, heat oil. Cook the turkey and onion 8-10 minutes or until meat is no longer pink; break up turkey into crumbles.
2. Transfer to a 5-qt. slow cooker; stir in seasonings. Add tomatoes, sweet peppers, chilies and garlic; stir in coffee and wine.
3. Cook, covered, on low 7-9 hours. Stir in beans; cook 15-20 minutes longer or until heated through. Top individual servings with avocado and green onions.

SPICY PUMPKIN & CORN SOUP

SLOW COOKER
SPINACH BEAN SOUP

As a college nursing professor, I always try to eat healthy. I was looking for a soup recipe that was easy to make and full of nutrients. This one hit the spot!

—BRENDA JEFFERS OTTUMWA, IA

PREP: 20 MIN. • **COOK:** 6¼ HOURS
MAKES: 8 SERVINGS (2 QUARTS)

- 3 cans (14½ ounces each) vegetable broth
- 1 can (15½ ounces) great northern beans, rinsed and drained
- 1 can (15 ounces) tomato puree
- ½ cup finely chopped onion
- ½ cup uncooked converted long grain rice
- 2 garlic cloves, minced
- 1 teaspoon dried basil
- ½ teaspoon salt
- ¼ teaspoon pepper
- 1 package (6 ounces) fresh baby spinach, coarsely chopped
- ¼ cup shredded Parmesan cheese

In a 4-qt. slow cooker, combine the first nine ingredients. Cover and cook on low for 6-7 hours or until heated through. Stir in spinach. Cover and cook for 15 minutes or until spinach is wilted. Sprinkle with cheese.

FREEZE OPTION *Before adding cheese, cool soup. Freeze soup in freezer containers. To use, partially thaw in refrigerator overnight. Heat through in a saucepan, stirring occasionally and adding a little more broth or water if necessary. Sprinkle each serving with cheese.*

SPINACH BEAN SOUP

TORTELLINI BAKE

Summer in New Hampshire brings plenty of fresh zucchini and squash. One year I had so much that I searched for new ways to prepare it. I came up with this, which is great as a side or a light meal.

—DONALD ROBERTS AMHERST, NH

PREP: 20 MIN. • **BAKE:** 20 MIN.
MAKES: 6-8 SERVINGS

- 1 package (10 ounces) refrigerated cheese tortellini
- 1 tablespoon olive oil
- 1 small zucchini, diced
- 1 yellow squash, diced
- 1 onion, diced
- 1 sweet red pepper, diced
- 1 teaspoon dried basil
- ½ teaspoon pepper
- ½ teaspoon salt
- 1 cup shredded part-skim mozzarella cheese
- 1 cup half-and-half cream

1. Cook the tortellini according to package directions. Meanwhile, heat oil in a skillet; cook zucchini, squash, onion, red pepper and seasonings until vegetables are crisp-tender.
2. Drain tortellini and rinse in hot water; combine with vegetable mixture, mozzarella and cream in a 1½-qt. baking dish.
3. Bake, uncovered, at 375° for 20 minutes or until heated through.
FREEZE OPTION *Cool unbaked casserole; cover and freeze. To use, partially thaw in refrigerator overnight. Remove from refrigerator 30 minutes before baking. Preheat oven to 375°. Bake the casserole as directed, increasing time as necessary to heat through and for a thermometer inserted in center to read 165°.*

SWEET AND SOUR ZUCCHINI

I have made this many times for potlucks. Everyone loves it, and it travels nicely, too. It's a wonderful way to use up the zucchini that we all have in such abundance in the summertime.

—MARIAN PLATT SEQUIM, WA

PREP: 10 MIN. + CHILLING
MAKES: 6-8 SERVINGS

- ¾ cup sugar
- 1 teaspoon salt
- ½ teaspoon pepper
- ⅓ cup vegetable oil
- ⅔ cup cider vinegar
- 2 tablespoons white wine vinegar
- 5 cups thinly sliced zucchini
- 1 small onion, chopped
- ½ cup chopped green pepper
- ½ cup chopped celery

In a large bowl, combine the first six ingredients; mix well. Stir in vegetables. Cover; refrigerate several hours or overnight.

SATISFYING TOMATO SOUP

I made up my own recipe to satisfy a craving for tomato soup. My sister loves this soup chunky-style, so she doesn't use a blender. Maybe you will prefer it that way, too!

—MARIAN BROWN MISSISSAUGA, ON

START TO FINISH: 30 MIN.
MAKES: 4 SERVINGS

- 2 teaspoons canola oil
- ¼ cup finely chopped onion
- ¼ cup finely chopped celery
- 2 cans (14½ ounces each) diced tomatoes, undrained
- 1½ cups water
- 2 teaspoons brown sugar
- ½ teaspoon salt
- ½ teaspoon dried basil
- ¼ teaspoon dried oregano
- ¼ teaspoon coarsely ground pepper

1. In a large saucepan, heat oil over medium-high heat. Add onion and celery; cook and stir 2-4 minutes or until tender. Add the remaining ingredients. Bring to a boil. Reduce heat; simmer, uncovered, 10 minutes to allow flavors to blend.

CRISPY POTATO PUFFS

2. Puree soup using an immersion blender. Or, cool soup slightly and puree in batches in a blender; return to pan and heat through.
FREEZE OPTION *Freeze cooled soup in freezer containers. To use, partially thaw in the refrigerator overnight. Heat through in a saucepan, stirring occasionally and adding a little water if necessary.*

CRISPY POTATO PUFFS

Crunchy cornflakes and sesame seeds surround a velvety potato filling in these adorable puffs. They are the perfect side dish. I keep a batch ready in the freezer.

—EVA TOMLINSON BRYAN, OH

PREP: 35 MIN. • **BAKE:** 10 MIN.
MAKES: 12 SERVINGS (2 PUFFS EACH)

- 4 pounds cubed peeled potatoes (about 11 cups)
- ½ cup 2% milk
- ¼ cup butter, cubed
- 1½ teaspoons salt
- ½ cup shredded cheddar cheese
- 1½ cups crushed cornflakes
- 6 tablespoons sesame seeds, toasted

1. Place potatoes in a large saucepan; add water to cover. Bring to a boil. Reduce heat; cook, uncovered, for 10-15 minutes or until tender. Drain; return to pan.
2. Mash the potatoes, gradually adding milk, butter and salt; stir in cheese. Transfer to a large bowl; refrigerate, covered, 2 hours or until firm enough to shape.
3. In a shallow dish, combine the cornflakes and sesame seeds. Shape the potato mixture into 1½-in. balls; roll in the cornflake mixture. Place on greased baking sheets. Bake for 7-9 minutes or until golden brown.
FREEZE OPTION *Place unbaked puffs on baking sheets; cover and freeze until firm. Transfer to resealable plastic freezer bags. Freeze up to 3 months. To use, preheat oven to 400°. Place frozen potato puffs on greased baking sheets. Bake 15-20 minutes or until golden brown and heated through.*

SAUSAGE STUFFING MUFFINS

Here's a clever new take on stuffing. You also can bake this stuffing in a greased baking dish for a more traditional presentation.

—TRICIA BIBB HARTSELLE, AL

PREP: 45 MIN. • **BAKE:** 20 MIN.
MAKES: 1½ DOZEN

- 1 pound bulk pork sausage
- 4 celery ribs, chopped
- 2 medium onions, chopped
- ¼ cup butter, cubed
- 1 package (14 ounces) crushed corn bread stuffing
- 2 medium apples, peeled and chopped
- 1 package (5 ounces) dried cranberries
- 1 cup chopped pecans
- 1 teaspoon salt
- 1 teaspoon pepper
- 2 to 3 cups reduced-sodium chicken broth
- 2 large eggs
- 2 teaspoons baking powder

1. Preheat oven to 375°. In a large skillet, cook sausage over medium heat until no longer pink; drain. Transfer to a large bowl; set aside.
2. In the same skillet, saute celery and onions in butter until tender. Transfer to bowl; add stuffing, apples, cranberries, pecans, salt and pepper. Stir in enough broth to reach desired moistness. Whisk eggs and baking powder; add to stuffing mixture.
3. Spoon into 18 greased muffin cups. Bake 20-25 minutes or until lightly browned. Cool 10 minutes. Run a knife around the edges of the muffin cups to loosen. Serve immediately.
FREEZE OPTION *Freeze cooled stuffing muffins in resealable plastic bags. To use, partially thaw in the refrigerator overnight. Place muffins on greased baking sheets, cover with foil and reheat in a preheated 375° oven for 6-10 minutes or until heated through.*

SWEET & SPICY ASIAN CHICKEN PETITES

SWEET & SPICY ASIAN CHICKEN PETITES

Using crescent roll dough, Sriracha and chili sauce, I came up with these tasty tidbits. Freeze a batch, and you'll have a great quick treat ready to reheat for drop-in guests.

—JEANETTE NELSON BRIDGEPORT, WV

PREP: 25 MIN. • **BAKE:** 10 MIN.
MAKES: 16 APPETIZERS

- 4 teaspoons olive oil, divided
- ⅓ cup finely chopped sweet red pepper
- 3 green onions, finely chopped
- 2 garlic cloves, minced
- 1 cup finely chopped cooked chicken breast
- 2 tablespoons island teriyaki sauce
- 1 tablespoon white grapefruit juice or water
- 1 tablespoon sesame oil
- 1 teaspoon Sriracha Asian hot chili sauce
- 1 tube (8 ounces) refrigerated crescent rolls
- 2 teaspoons sesame seeds
  Sweet chili sauce

1. Preheat oven to 375°. In a large skillet, heat 2 teaspoons olive oil over medium-high heat. Add red pepper, green onions and garlic; cook and stir 3-5 minutes or until vegetables are tender. Stir in chicken, teriyaki sauce, grapefruit juice, sesame oil and hot chili sauce. Remove from heat; cool slightly.
2. Unroll crescent dough into one long rectangle; press perforations to seal. Roll dough into a 12-in. square; cut into 16 3-in. squares. Place 1 tablespoon of the chicken mixture in the center of each square. Bring edges of dough over filling, pinching seams to seal; shape into a ball.
3. Place balls on ungreased baking sheets, seam side down. Brush tops with remaining olive oil; sprinkle with sesame seeds. Bake 10-12 minutes or until golden brown. Serve warm with sweet chili sauce.
FREEZE OPTION *Freeze cooled appetizers in resealable plastic freezer bags. To use, reheat appetizers on a baking sheet in a preheated 375° oven until heated through.*

SLOW COOKER SPLIT PEA SOUP

Whenever I have leftover ham in the fridge, I like to make this soup. Just throw the ingredients in the slow cooker, turn it on and dinner is done!

—**PAMELA CHAMBERS** WEST COLUMBIA, SC

PREP: 15 MIN. • **COOK:** 8 HOURS
MAKES: 8 SERVINGS

- 1 package (16 ounces) dried green split peas, rinsed
- 2 cups cubed fully cooked ham
- 1 large onion, chopped
- 1 cup julienned or chopped carrots
- 3 garlic cloves, minced
- ½ teaspoon dried rosemary, crushed
- ½ teaspoon dried thyme
- 1 carton (32 ounces) reduced-sodium chicken broth
- 2 cups water

In a 4- or 5-qt. slow cooker, combine all of the ingredients. Cover and cook on low for 8-10 hours or until the peas are tender.

FREEZE OPTION *Freeze cooled soup in freezer containers. To use, thaw overnight in the refrigerator. Heat through in a saucepan over medium heat, stirring occasionally.*

SLOW COOKER SPLIT PEA SOUP

HOT ITALIAN SAUSAGE SOUP

HOT ITALIAN SAUSAGE SOUP

I'm part owner of a small tavern, and on Saturdays we provide soups and deli sandwiches free of charge. Our patrons love this one loaded with zesty sausage and an array of veggies. A hint of brown sugar balances the heat with a little bit of sweetness, making it a real crowd-pleaser.

—**DAN BUTE** OTTAWA, IL

START TO FINISH: 25 MIN.
MAKES: 4 SERVINGS

- 1 pound bulk hot Italian sausage
- 1 can (14½ ounces) Italian stewed tomatoes
- 1 can (8 ounces) tomato sauce
- 1 cup frozen Italian vegetables
- ¾ cup julienned green, sweet red and/or yellow pepper
- ¼ cup chopped onion
- ¼ cup white wine or chicken broth
- 1 teaspoon brown sugar
- 1 teaspoon minced fresh parsley
- ½ teaspoon Italian seasoning
- ⅛ teaspoon salt
- ⅛ teaspoon pepper

1. In a large skillet, cook sausage over medium heat until no longer pink.
2. Meanwhile, in a large saucepan, combine the remaining ingredients. Bring to a boil. Reduce heat; cover and simmer for 10 minutes or until vegetables are tender.
3. Drain sausage; add to soup and heat through.

FREEZE OPTION *Cool soup and transfer to freezer containers. Freeze up to 3 months. To use, thaw in the refrigerator overnight. Transfer to a saucepan. Cover and cook over medium heat until heated through.*

BEEFY ENTREES

Whether in casseroles, stews, sandwiches, roasts or any number of dishes, beef makes a hearty and satisfying main course. Here are some great recipes for you to make and serve year-round!

TASTY BURRITOS, P. 43

CHIPOTLE SHREDDED BEEF

CHIPOTLE SHREDDED BEEF

The basic recipe for this spicy shredded beef has it served over rice, but you can use it in so many ways! It's delicious all rolled up in a tortilla, served with corn salsa and eaten as a burrito, over mashed potatoes or in buns as a hot sandwich.

—**DARCY WILLIAMS** OMAHA, NE

PREP: 25 MIN. • **COOK:** 8 HOURS
MAKES: 10 SERVINGS

- 1 teaspoon canola oil
- 1 small onion, chopped
- 1 can (28 ounces) diced tomatoes, undrained
- ¼ cup cider vinegar
- ¼ cup chopped chipotle peppers in adobo sauce plus 2 teaspoons sauce
- 6 garlic cloves, minced
- 2 tablespoons brown sugar
- 2 bay leaves
- ½ teaspoon ground cumin
- ½ teaspoon paprika
- ½ teaspoon pepper
- ¼ teaspoon ground cinnamon
- 1 boneless beef chuck roast (2½ pounds)
- 5 cups cooked brown rice
   Shredded reduced-fat cheddar cheese and reduced-fat sour cream, optional

1. In a large skillet coated with cooking spray, heat oil over medium-high heat. Add onion; cook and stir for 2-3 minutes or until tender. Stir in tomatoes, vinegar, peppers with sauce, garlic, brown sugar, bay leaves and spices. Bring to a boil. Reduce heat; simmer, uncovered, 4-6 minutes or until thickened.
2. Place roast in a 5-qt. slow cooker; add tomato mixture. Cook, covered, on low for 8-10 hours or until the meat is tender.
3. Discard bay leaves. Remove the roast; cool slightly. Skim fat from the cooking juices. Shred beef with two forks. Return meat and cooking juices to slow cooker; heat through. Serve with rice. If desired, top with cheese and sour cream.

FREEZE IT

Freeze cooled meat mixture and juices in freezer containers. To use, partially thaw in refrigerator overnight. Heat through in a saucepan, stirring occasionally and adding a little water if necessary.

BAVARIAN POT ROAST

ZUCCHINI PIZZA CASSEROLE

Three things make this tasty casserole tops with our family: My husband has a hearty appetite, our two kids never tire of pizza and I grow lots of zucchini! Once you've tried it, you may even plant more zucchini next summer!

—**LYNN BERNSTETTER**
WHITE BEAR LAKE, MN

PREP: 20 MIN. • **BAKE:** 40 MIN.
MAKES: 8 SERVINGS

- 4 **cups shredded unpeeled zucchini**
- ½ **teaspoon salt**
- 2 **large eggs**
- ½ **cup grated Parmesan cheese**
- 2 **cups shredded part-skim mozzarella cheese, divided**
- 1 **cup shredded cheddar cheese, divided**
- 1 **pound ground beef**
- ½ **cup chopped onion**
- 1 **can (15 ounces) Italian tomato sauce**
- 1 **medium sweet red pepper, chopped**

1. Preheat oven to 400°. Place zucchini in colander; sprinkle with salt. Let stand 10 minutes, then squeeze out moisture.
2. Combine zucchini with eggs, Parmesan and half of mozzarella and cheddar cheeses. Press into a greased 13x9-in. or 3-qt. baking dish. Bake for 20 minutes.
3. Meanwhile, in a large saucepan, cook beef and onion over medium heat, crumbling beef, until meat is no longer pink. Drain the beef and add tomato sauce. Spoon the beef mixture over the zucchini mixture. Sprinkle with remaining cheeses, and add red pepper. Bake until heated through, about 20 minutes longer.
FREEZE OPTION *Cool baked casserole; cover and freeze. To use, partially thaw in the refrigerator overnight. Remove from refrigerator 30 minutes before baking. Preheat oven to 350°. Unwrap casserole; reheat on a lower oven rack until heated through and a thermometer inserted in center reads 165°.*

BAVARIAN POT ROAST

Because all my grandparents were German, it's no wonder that so many Bavarian recipes have been handed down to me! This is one of my favorites.
—**SUSAN ROBERTSON** HAMILTON, OH

PREP: 15 MIN. • **COOK:** 2¾ HOURS
MAKES: 8-10 SERVINGS

- 1 **boneless beef chuck pot roast (about 3 pounds)**
- 2 **tablespoons canola oil**
- 1¼ **cups water**
- ¾ **cup beer or beef broth**
- 1 **can (8 ounces) tomato sauce**
- ½ **cup chopped onion**
- 2 **tablespoons sugar**
- 1 **tablespoon vinegar**
- 2 **teaspoons salt**
- 1 **teaspoon ground cinnamon**
- 1 **bay leaf**
- ½ **teaspoon pepper**
- ½ **teaspoon ground ginger**
  Cornstarch and water, optional

1. In a Dutch oven, brown roast on all sides in hot oil. Combine water, beer, tomato sauce, onion, sugar, vinegar, salt, cinnamon, bay leaf, pepper and ginger. Pour over meat and bring to a boil. Reduce heat; cover and simmer until meat is tender, 2½ to 3 hours.
2. Remove meat. Discard bay leaf. If desired, thicken juices with a slurry of cornstarch and water.
FREEZE OPTION *Place sliced pot roast in freezer containers; top with cooking juices. Cool and freeze. To use, partially thaw in refrigerator overnight. Microwave, covered, on high in a microwave-safe dish until heated through, gently stirring and adding a little broth if necessary.*

ZUCCHINI PIZZA CASSEROLE

BEEF TENDERLOIN SUPREME

A wine and mushroom gravy gives fantastic flavor to tenderloin slices. It's perfect for entertaining because the meat marinates overnight.

—BARB LAABS IRON RIDGE, WI

PREP: 30 MIN. + MARINATING
BAKE: 45 MIN. + STANDING
MAKES: 12 SERVINGS (3 CUPS SAUCE)

- 4 **cups beef broth**
- 2 **cups Burgundy wine or additional beef broth**
- ¼ **cup tomato paste**
- 4 **teaspoons minced fresh parsley**
- 4 **teaspoons white wine vinegar**
- 2 **teaspoons dried thyme**
- 1 **teaspoon pepper**
- 1 **beef tenderloin roast (4 pounds)**
- 2 **cups sliced fresh mushrooms**
- 1 **medium onion, chopped**
- 6 **tablespoons butter**
- 3 **tablespoons all-purpose flour**

1. In a large bowl, combine the first seven ingredients. Place beef in a large resealable plastic bag; add half of the marinade. Seal bag and turn to coat. Refrigerate for 8 hours or overnight. Cover and refrigerate remaining marinade for sauce.

2. Drain and discard marinade. Place the tenderloin on a rack in a shallow roasting pan. Bake, uncovered, at 425° for 45-60 minutes or until meat reaches desired doneness (for medium-rare, a meat thermometer should read 145°; medium, 160°; well-done, 170°). Let stand for 10 minutes before slicing.

3. For sauce, in a large skillet, saute mushrooms and onion in butter until tender. Stir in flour until blended; gradually add the reserved marinade. Bring to a boil; cook and stir for 2 minutes or until thickened. Serve with beef.

WINTERTIME BRAISED BEEF STEW

This wonderful beef stew makes an easy Sunday meal. It's even better a day or two later, so we make a double batch for leftovers.

—MICHAELA ROSENTHAL
WOODLAND HILLS, CA

PREP: 40 MIN. • **BAKE:** 2 HOURS
MAKES: 8 SERVINGS (2 QUARTS)

- 2 **pounds boneless beef sirloin steak or chuck roast, cut into 1-inch pieces**
- 2 **tablespoons all-purpose flour**
- 2 **teaspoons Montreal steak seasoning**
- 2 **tablespoons olive oil, divided**
- 1 **large onion, chopped**
- 2 **celery ribs, chopped**
- 2 **medium parsnips, peeled and cut into 1½-inch pieces**
- 2 **medium carrots, peeled and cut into 1½-inch pieces**
- 2 **garlic cloves, minced**
- 1 **can (14½ ounces) diced tomatoes, undrained**
- 1 **cup dry red wine or reduced-sodium beef broth**
- 2 **tablespoons red currant jelly**
- 2 **bay leaves**
- 2 **fresh oregano sprigs**
- 1 **can (15 ounces) white kidney or cannellini beans, rinsed and drained**
  Minced fresh parsley, optional

1. Preheat oven to 350°. Toss beef with flour and steak seasoning.
2. In an ovenproof Dutch oven, heat 1 tablespoon oil over medium heat. Brown beef in batches; remove with a slotted spoon.
3. In same pan, heat the remaining oil over medium heat. Add onion, celery, parsnips and carrots; cook and stir until onion is tender. Add garlic; cook 1 minute longer. Stir in tomatoes, wine, jelly, bay leaves, oregano and beef; bring to a boil.
4. Bake, covered, 1½ hours. Stir in beans; bake, covered, 30-40 minutes longer or until beef and vegetables are tender. Remove bay leaves and oregano sprigs. If desired, sprinkle with parsley.

GREEK PASTA BAKE

The subtle sweetness of cinnamon complements tangy lemon and savory herbs in this pasta bake with a Mediterranean taste.

—CAROL STEVENS BASYE, VA

PREP: 40 MIN. • **BAKE:** 1 HOUR
MAKES: 6 SERVINGS

- ½ pound ground beef
- ½ pound ground lamb
- 1 large onion, chopped
- 4 garlic cloves, minced
- 3 teaspoons dried oregano
- 1 teaspoon dried basil
- ½ teaspoon salt
- ¼ teaspoon pepper
- ¼ teaspoon dried thyme
- 1 can (15 ounces) tomato sauce
- 1 can (14½ ounces) diced tomatoes, undrained
- 1 tablespoon lemon juice
- 1 teaspoon sugar
- ¼ teaspoon ground cinnamon
- 2 cups uncooked rigatoni or large tube pasta
- 4 ounces feta cheese, crumbled

1. In a large skillet, cook beef and lamb over medium heat until no longer pink; drain. Stir in onion, garlic, oregano, basil, salt, pepper and thyme. Add tomato sauce, tomatoes and lemon juice. Bring to a boil. Reduce heat; simmer, uncovered, for 20 minutes, stirring occasionally.

2. Stir in sugar and cinnamon. Simmer, uncovered, 15 minutes longer.

3. Meanwhile, cook the pasta according to package directions; drain. Stir into the meat mixture.

4. Transfer to a greased 2-qt. baking dish. Sprinkle with feta cheese. Cover and bake at 325° for 45 minutes. Uncover; bake 15 minutes longer or until heated through.

FREEZE OPTION *Cool unbaked casserole; cover and freeze. To use, partially thaw in the refrigerator overnight. Remove from refrigerator 30 minutes before baking. Preheat oven to 325°. Bake the casserole as directed, increasing time as necessary to heat through and for a thermometer inserted in center to read 165°.*

LONDON BROIL

I received this delicious recipe from my mother-in-law. Prepared on the grill, it's a real treat during warm-weather months.

—SUSAN WILKINS LOS OLIVOS, CA

PREP: 10 MIN. + MARINATING
GRILL: 15 MIN.
MAKES: 6 SERVINGS

- ½ cup water
- ¼ cup red wine vinegar
- 2 tablespoons canola oil
- 1 tablespoon tomato paste
- 1½ teaspoons garlic salt, divided
- 1 teaspoon dried thyme, divided
- ½ teaspoon pepper, divided
- 1 bay leaf
- 1 beef flank steak (1½ pounds)

1. In a small bowl, whisk water, vinegar, oil, tomato paste, 1 teaspoon garlic salt, ½ teaspoon thyme and ¼ teaspoon pepper; add bay leaf. Pour into a large resealable plastic bag.

2. Score the surface of the steak, making diamond shapes ¼ in. deep; add to marinade. Seal bag and turn to coat; refrigerate for 3 hours or overnight, turning occasionally.

3. Drain and discard marinade. Pat steak dry with paper towels. Combine the remaining garlic salt, thyme and pepper; rub over both sides of steak.

4. Grill steak, covered, over medium-hot heat or broil 4 in. from the grill for 6-8 minutes on each side or until a meat thermometer reaches desired doneness (for medium-rare, a meat thermometer should read 145°; medium, 160°; well-done, 170°). Let stand for 5 minutes. Thinly slice across the grain.

GREEK PASTA BAKE

MACHACA BEEF DIP SANDWICHES

EASY MARINATED FLANK STEAK

A friend gave me this recipe 15 years ago.
Even now, when my family makes steak
on the grill, this is the recipe we use. It's
a must when we're having company.
—**DEBBIE BONCZEK** TARIFFVILLE, CT

EASY MARINATED FLANK STEAK

A friend gave me this recipe 15 years ago. Even now, when my family makes steak on the grill, this is the recipe we use. It's a must when we're having company.

—**DEBBIE BONCZEK** TARIFFVILLE, CT

PREP: 10 MIN. + MARINATING
GRILL: 15 MIN.
MAKES: 8 SERVINGS

- 3 tablespoons ketchup
- 1 tablespoon chopped onion
- 1 tablespoon canola oil
- 1 teaspoon brown sugar
- 1 teaspoon Worcestershire sauce
- 1 garlic clove, minced
- ⅛ teaspoon pepper
- 1 beef flank steak (about 2 pounds)

1. In a large resealable plastic bag, combine the first seven ingredients. Add beef; seal bag and turn to coat. Refrigerate 8 hours or overnight.
2. Drain beef, discarding marinade. Moisten a paper towel with cooking oil; using long-handled tongs, rub on grill rack to coat lightly.
3. Grill beef, covered, over medium heat or broil 4 in. from the heat for 6-8 minutes on each side or until meat reaches desired doneness (for medium-rare, a thermometer should read 145°; medium, 160°; well-done, 170°). To serve, thinly slice across the grain.
FREEZE OPTION *Freeze beef with marinade in a resealable plastic freezer bag. To use, thaw in the refrigerator overnight. Drain beef, discarding marinade. Grill as directed.*

MACHACA BEEF DIP SANDWICHES

The winning combo of beef, cumin, chili powder and the spicy, smoky heat of chipotle peppers makes these sandwiches a perfect game-day meal!

—**KAROL EZELL** NACOGDOCHES, TX

PREP: 20 MIN. • **COOK:** 8 HOURS
MAKES: 6 SERVINGS

- 1 boneless beef chuck roast (2 to 3 pounds)
- 1 large sweet onion, thinly sliced
- 1 can (14½ ounces) reduced-sodium beef broth
- ½ cup water
- 3 chipotle peppers in adobo sauce, chopped
- 1 tablespoon adobo sauce
- 1 envelope au jus gravy mix
- 1 tablespoon Creole seasoning
- 1 tablespoon chili powder
- 2 teaspoons ground cumin
- 6 French rolls, split
  Guacamole and salsa, optional

1. Place roast in a 3- to 4-qt. slow cooker; top with onion. Combine beef broth, water, chipotle peppers, adobo sauce, gravy mix, Creole seasoning, chili powder and cumin; pour over meat. Cover, cook on low 8-10 hours or until meat is tender.
2. Remove roast; cool slightly. Skim fat from cooking juices. Shred beef with two forks and return meat to slow cooker; heat through. Using a slotted spoon, place meat on rolls. Serve with the cooking juices on the side and top with guacamole or salsa if desired.
FREEZE OPTION *Freeze individual portions of cool meat mixture and juice in freezer containers. To use, partially thaw in refrigerator overnight. Heat through in a saucepan, stirring occasionally.*
NOTES *Wear disposable gloves when cutting hot peppers; the oils can burn skin. Avoid touching your face. The following spices may be substituted for 1 tablespoon Creole seasoning: ¾ teaspoon each salt, garlic powder and paprika; and a pinch each of dried thyme, ground cumin and cayenne pepper.*

EASY MARINATED FLANK STEAK

CUBAN ROPA VIEJA

This recipe offers a great authentic Cuban taste that can be prepared at home. I love having this as a go-to recipe for a weeknight meal.

—MELISSA PELKEY HASS WALESKA, GA

PREP: 25 MIN. • **COOK:** 7 HOURS
MAKES: 8 SERVINGS

- 6 **bacon strips, chopped**
- 2 **beef flank steaks (1 pound each), cut in half**
- 1 **can (28 ounces) crushed tomatoes**
- 2 **cups beef stock**
- 1 **can (6 ounces) tomato paste**
- 5 **garlic cloves, minced**
- 1 **tablespoon ground cumin**
- 2 **teaspoons dried thyme**
- ¾ **teaspoon salt**
- ½ **teaspoon pepper**
- 1 **medium onion, thinly sliced**
- 1 **medium sweet red pepper, sliced**
- 1 **medium green pepper, sliced**
- ¼ **cup minced fresh cilantro**
  Hot cooked rice

1. In a large skillet, cook bacon over medium heat until crisp, stirring occasionally. Remove with a slotted spoon; drain on paper towels.

2. In same skillet, heat drippings over medium-high heat; brown steak in batches. Transfer meat and bacon to a 5- or 6-qt. slow cooker. In a large bowl, combine tomatoes, beef stock, tomato paste, garlic, seasonings and vegetables; pour over the meat. Cook, covered, on low 7-9 hours or until the meat is tender. Shred beef with two forks; return to slow cooker. Stir in cilantro. Remove with a slotted spoon; serve with rice.

FREEZE OPTION *Freeze cooled meat mixture in freezer containers. To use, partially thaw in the refrigerator overnight. Microwave, covered, on high in a microwave-safe dish until heated through, gently stirring and adding a little stock or water if necessary.*

CUBAN ROPA VIEJA

MAKEOVER EASY BEEF-STUFFED SHELLS

Enjoy the convenience of this make-ahead dish or bake and serve it right away. Either way, it's a healthy version of a traditional (but saturated-fat-laden) favorite. Give it a try!

—BLAIR LONERGAN ROCHELLE, VA

PREP: 45 MIN. + CHILLING • **BAKE:** 45 MIN.
MAKES: 10 SERVINGS

- 20 uncooked jumbo pasta shells
- 1 pound lean ground beef (90% lean)
- 1 large onion, chopped
- 1 medium green pepper, chopped
- 1¼ cups reduced-fat ricotta cheese
- 1½ cups shredded reduced-fat Italian cheese blend, divided
- ¼ cup grated Parmesan cheese
- ¼ cup prepared pesto
- 1 large egg, lightly beaten
- 1 can (14½ ounces) Italian diced tomatoes, undrained
- 1 can (8 ounces) no-salt-added tomato sauce
- 1 teaspoon Italian seasoning

1. Cook pasta according to package directions for al dente; drain and rinse in cold water. In a large skillet, cook beef, onion and green pepper over medium heat until the meat is no longer pink; drain. In a large bowl, combine ricotta cheese, 1 cup Italian cheese blend, Parmesan cheese, pesto, egg and half of the beef mixture.

2. In a small bowl, combine tomatoes, tomato sauce and Italian seasoning. Spread ¾ cup into a 13x9-in. baking dish coated with cooking spray. Spoon the cheese mixture into the pasta shells; place in baking dish. Combine the remaining beef mixture and tomato mixture; spoon over the shells. Sprinkle with the remaining cheese. Cover and refrigerate overnight.

3. Remove from the refrigerator 30 minutes before baking. Cover and bake at 350° for 40 minutes. Uncover; bake 5-10 minutes longer or until cheese is melted.

MAKEOVER EASY BEEF-STUFFED SHELLS

SLOW-COOKED HUNGARIAN GOULASH

The rich creamy sauce in this dish is certain to satisfy the pickiest goulash lovers! This recipe is great for potluck suppers, too. If you like, use a little fresh parsley to add flavor and color to the finished dish.

—JACKIE KOHN DULUTH, MN

PREP: 15 MIN. • **COOK:** 8 HOURS
MAKES: 6-8 SERVINGS

- 2 pounds beef top round steak, cut into 1-inch cubes
- 1 cup chopped onion
- 2 tablespoons all-purpose flour
- 1½ teaspoons paprika
- 1 teaspoon garlic salt
- ½ teaspoon pepper
- 1 can (14½ ounces) diced tomatoes, undrained
- 1 bay leaf
- 1 cup sour cream
  Hot cooked egg noodles

1. Place beef and onion in a 3-qt. slow cooker. Combine flour, paprika, garlic salt and pepper; sprinkle over the beef and stir to coat. Stir in tomatoes; add bay leaf. Cover and cook on low for 8-10 hours or until the meat is tender.

2. Discard the bay leaf. Just before serving, stir in sour cream; heat through. Serve with noodles.

FREEZE OPTION *Before adding the sour cream, cool the stew. Freeze in freezer containers. To use, partially thaw in refrigerator overnight. Heat through in a saucepan, stirring occasionally and adding a little broth if necessary. Remove from heat; stir in sour cream.*

✱

DID YOU KNOW? Goulash is a type of Hungarian stew, made with meat and vegetables and seasoned with paprika. It's the paprika that sets goulash apart from other types of stew!

TASTY BURRITOS

My cousin is of Mexican heritage, and I've watched her make these crunchy burritos for years. The very first time I made them for my own family, they became an instant favorite meal.
—**DEBI LANE** CHATTANOOGA, TN

START TO FINISH: 30 MIN.
MAKES: 6 SERVINGS

- 1 pound ground beef
- 1 envelope taco seasoning
- 1 can (16 ounces) refried beans
- 6 flour tortillas (12 inches), warmed
- 1 cup shredded Colby-Monterey Jack cheese
- 4 teaspoons canola oil
  Sour cream and salsa

1. In a large skillet, cook beef over medium heat until no longer pink; drain. Stir in taco seasoning. In a small saucepan, cook refried beans over medium-low heat for 2-3 minutes or until heated through.

2. Spoon about 1/3 cup of the beans off-center on each tortilla; top with 1/4 cup of the beef mixture. Sprinkle with cheese. Fold sides and ends of tortillas over the filling and roll up.

3. In a large skillet over medium-high heat, brown burritos in oil on all sides. Serve with sour cream and salsa.

FREEZE OPTION *Individually wrap cooled burritos in paper towels and foil; freeze in a resealable plastic freezer bag. To use, remove foil; place paper towel-wrapped burrito on a microwave-safe plate. Microwave on high 3-4 minutes or until heated through, turning once. Let stand 20 seconds.*

TASTY BURRITOS

JAMAICAN-STYLE BEEF STEW

This delicious stew makes a hearty supper with a lighter touch. It's so flavorful, you won't want to stop at just one bowlful!
—**JAMES HAYES** RIDGECREST, CA

PREP: 25 MIN. • **COOK:** 1¼ HOURS
MAKES: 5 SERVINGS

- 1 tablespoon canola oil
- 1 tablespoon sugar
- 1½ pounds beef top sirloin steak, cut into ¾-inch cubes
- 5 plum tomatoes, finely chopped
- 3 large carrots, cut into ½-inch slices
- 3 celery ribs, cut into ½-inch slices
- 4 green onions, chopped
- ¾ cup reduced-sodium beef broth
- ¼ cup barbecue sauce
- ¼ cup reduced-sodium soy sauce
- 2 tablespoons steak sauce
- 1 tablespoon garlic powder
- 1 teaspoon dried thyme
- ¼ teaspoon ground allspice
- ¼ teaspoon pepper
- ⅛ teaspoon hot pepper sauce
- 1 tablespoon cornstarch
- 2 tablespoons cold water
  Hot cooked rice or mashed potatoes, optional

1. In a Dutch oven, heat oil over medium-high heat. Add sugar; cook and stir for 1 minute or until lightly browned. Add beef and brown on all sides.

2. Stir in vegetables, broth, barbecue sauce, soy sauce, steak sauce and seasonings. Bring to a boil. Reduce heat; cover and simmer for 1 to 1¼ hours or until meat and vegetables are tender.

3. Combine cornstarch and water until smooth; stir into stew. Bring to a boil; cook and stir for 2 minutes or until thickened. Serve with rice or potatoes if desired.

FREEZE OPTION *Freeze cooled stew in freezer containers. To use, partially thaw in the refrigerator overnight. Heat through in a saucepan, stirring occasionally and adding a little water if necessary.*

FREEZE IT

Cover and freeze unbaked pie. To use, remove
from the freezer 30 minutes before baking.
Cover edges of crust loosely with foil; place on
a baking sheet. Bake at 425° for 30 minutes.
Reduce heat to 350°; remove foil. Bake
55-60 minutes longer or until golden brown.

SPICY BEAN AND BEEF PIE

My daughter helped me create this recipe one day when we wanted a one-dish meal that is something other than a casserole. Any extras microwave nicely for lunch the next day, too.

—DEBRA DOHY NEWCOMERSTOWN, OH

PREP: 20 MIN. • **BAKE:** 30 MIN.
MAKES: 8 SERVINGS

- 1 **pound ground beef**
- 2 **to 3 garlic cloves, minced**
- 1 **can (11½ ounces) condensed bean with bacon soup, undiluted**
- 1 **jar (16 ounces) thick and chunky picante sauce, divided**
- ¼ **cup cornstarch**
- 1 **tablespoon chopped fresh parsley**
- 1 **teaspoon paprika**
- 1 **teaspoon salt**
- ¼ **teaspoon pepper**
- 1 **can (16 ounces) kidney beans, rinsed and drained**
- 1 **can (15 ounces) black beans, rinsed and drained**
- 2 **cups shredded cheddar cheese, divided**
- ¾ **cup sliced green onions, divided**
  Pastry for double-crust pie (10 inches)
- 1 **cup (8 ounces) sour cream**
- 1 **can (2¼ ounces) sliced ripe olives, drained**

1. In a large skillet, cook beef over medium heat until beef is no longer pink. Add garlic; cook 1 minute longer. Drain.

2. In a large bowl, combine the soup, 1 cup of picante sauce, cornstarch, parsley, paprika, salt and pepper. Fold in the beans, 1½ cups of cheese, ½ cup onions and the beef mixture.

3. Line a 9-in. deep-dish pie plate with bottom pastry; fill with bean mixture. Top with remaining pastry; seal and flute edges. Cut slits in top crust.

4. Bake at 425° for 30-35 minutes or until lightly browned. Let stand for 5 minutes before cutting. Garnish with sour cream, olives and remaining picante sauce, cheese and onions.

MUFFIN-CUP CHEDDAR BEEF PIES

My kids love these beef rolls so much that I always make extra because they heat up so quickly. I give the kids their choice of dipping sauces—spaghetti sauce or ranch dressing are the top picks.

—KIMBERLY FARMER WICHITA, KS

PREP: 25 MIN. + STANDING • **BAKE:** 20 MIN.
MAKES: 20 MEAT PIES

- 2 **loaves (1 pound each) frozen bread dough**
- 2 **pounds ground beef**
- 1 **can (8 ounces) mushroom stems and pieces, drained**
- 1¼ **cups shredded cheddar cheese**
- 1½ **teaspoons Italian seasoning**
- 1 **teaspoon garlic powder**
- ½ **teaspoon salt**
- ¼ **teaspoon pepper**
  Spaghetti sauce, warmed

1. Let the dough stand at room temperature 30 minutes or until softened. Preheat oven to 350°. Meanwhile, in a Dutch oven, cook beef over medium heat 12-15 minutes or until no longer pink, breaking into crumbles; drain. Stir in mushrooms, cheese and seasonings.

2. Divide each loaf into 10 portions; roll each into a 4-in. circle. Top with ¼ cup filling; bring edges of dough up over filling and pinch to seal.

3. Place meat pies in greased muffin cups, seam side down. Bake for 20-25 minutes or until golden brown. Serve with spaghetti sauce.

FREEZE OPTION *Freeze cooled beef pies in a resealable plastic freezer bag. To use, reheat beef pies on greased baking sheets in a preheated 350° oven until heated through.*

MUFFIN-CUP CHEDDAR BEEF PIES

SIRLOIN IN WINE SAUCE

This recipe is a family favorite as well as a fabulously easy company dish. Tender sirloin in a hearty mushroom-wine sauce is fantastic over pasta.

—BARBARA KAMM WILMINGTON, DE

START TO FINISH: 30 MIN.
MAKES: 4 SERVINGS

- 2 tablespoons all-purpose flour
- ⅛ teaspoon ground mustard
- 1 pound beef top sirloin steak, thinly sliced
- 2 tablespoons butter
- 1 can (10½ ounces) condensed beef consomme, undiluted
- ½ cup dry red wine or beef broth
- 1 jar (4½ ounces) sliced mushrooms, drained
- ¼ cup chopped green onions
- 1 teaspoon Worcestershire sauce
  Hot cooked linguine

1. In a large resealable plastic bag, combine flour and mustard. Add beef, a few pieces at a time, and shake to coat.

2. In a large skillet, brown beef in butter. Add consomme and wine. Stir in mushrooms, onions and Worcestershire sauce. Bring to a boil. Reduce heat; simmer, uncovered, for 10-15 minutes or until sauce is thickened. Serve with linguine.

FREEZE OPTION *Cool beef mixture. Freeze in freezer containers. To use, partially thaw in the refrigerator overnight. Heat through slowly in a covered skillet until a thermometer inserted in beef reads 165°, stirring occasionally and adding a little broth or water if necessary. Serve as directed.*

SIRLOIN IN WINE SAUCE

TOP-RATED ITALIAN POT ROAST

SLOW COOKER

TOP-RATED ITALIAN POT ROAST

I'm always collecting recipes from newspapers and magazines, and this one just sounded too good not to try! You'll love the blend of wholesome ingredients and aromatic spices.

—KAREN BURDELL LAFAYETTE, CO

PREP: 30 MIN. • **COOK:** 6 HOURS
MAKES: 8 SERVINGS

- 1 cinnamon stick (3 inches)
- 6 whole peppercorns
- 4 whole cloves
- 3 whole allspice berries
- 2 teaspoons olive oil
- 1 boneless beef chuck roast (2 pounds)
- 2 celery ribs, sliced
- 2 medium carrots, sliced
- 1 large onion, chopped
- 4 garlic cloves, minced
- 1 cup dry sherry or reduced-sodium beef broth
- 1 can (28 ounces) crushed tomatoes
- ¼ teaspoon salt
  Hot cooked egg noodles and minced parsley, optional

1. Place cinnamon, peppercorns, cloves and allspice on a double thickness of cheesecloth. Gather corners of cloth to enclose spices; tie securely with string.

2. In a large skillet, heat the oil over medium-high heat. Brown roast on all sides; transfer to a 4-qt. slow cooker. Add celery, carrots and spice bag.

3. Add onion to same skillet; cook and stir until tender. Add garlic; cook 1 minute longer. Add sherry, stirring to loosen browned bits from pan. Bring to a boil; cook and stir until liquid is reduced to ⅔ cup. Stir in tomatoes and salt; pour over roast and vegetables.

4. Cook, covered, on low 6-7 hours or until meat and vegetables are tender. Remove roast from slow cooker; keep warm. Discard spice bag; skim fat from sauce. Serve roast and sauce with noodles and parsley if desired.

FREEZE OPTION *Place sliced pot roast in freezer containers; top with sauce. Cool and freeze. To use, partially thaw in the refrigerator overnight. Heat through in a covered saucepan, stirring gently and adding a little broth if necessary.*

MOIST & SAVORY MEAT LOAF

Stop searching for a go-to meat loaf recipe. Your family will be delighted with this mixture of beef, pork and sauteed onion with a sweet-and-tangy sauce baked on the top. Cheese crackers are the secret ingredient in this one.
—*TASTE OF HOME* **TEST KITCHEN**

PREP: 20 MIN.
BAKE: 1¼ HOURS + STANDING
MAKES: 8 SERVINGS

- 1 medium onion, chopped
- 2 teaspoons canola oil
- 2 large eggs, lightly beaten
- ⅓ cup 2% milk
- 2 teaspoons Worcestershire sauce
- 2 teaspoons Dijon mustard
- ⅔ cup finely crushed cheese crackers
- 1 teaspoon salt
- ½ teaspoon pepper
- ½ teaspoon dried thyme
- 1½ pounds ground beef
- ½ pound ground pork
- ¾ cup ketchup
- ¼ cup packed brown sugar

1. Saute onion in oil in a small skillet until tender. Let cool to room temperature.
2. In a large bowl, combine the eggs, milk, Worcestershire sauce, mustard, crackers, salt, pepper, thyme and onion. Crumble beef and pork over mixture and mix well. Shape into a loaf; place in a greased 11x7-in. baking dish.
3. Bake, uncovered, at 350° for 1 hour. Combine ketchup and brown sugar; spread half of sauce over meat loaf. Bake 15-20 minutes longer or until no pink remains and a thermometer reads 160°. Let stand for 10 minutes before slicing. Serve with remaining sauce.
FREEZE OPTION *Bake meat loaf without sauce. Securely wrap and freeze cooled meat loaf in plastic wrap and foil. To use, partially thaw in refrigerator overnight. Unwrap meat loaf and place in a greased shallow baking pan. Prepare sauce as directed; spread half of sauce over meat loaf. Reheat meat loaf in a preheated 350° oven until heated through and a thermometer inserted in center reads 165°. Serve with remaining sauce.*

MOIST & SAVORY MEAT LOAF

PROVOLONE BEEF PASTRY POCKETS

My children always make sure they're home when they find out we're having these pockets for dinner. This is also a smart way to use leftover pot roast.
—**KAREN BURKETT** RESEDA, CA

PREP: 25 MIN. • **BAKE:** 20 MIN.
MAKES: 6 SERVINGS

- 1 tablespoon butter
- 2 cups finely chopped fresh mushrooms
- 1 small onion, finely chopped
- 1 package (17 ounces) refrigerated beef roast au jus
- 1 large egg
- 1 tablespoon water
- 1 package (17.3 ounces) frozen puff pastry, thawed
- 6 slices provolone cheese

1. Preheat oven to 425°. In a large skillet, heat butter over medium-high heat. Add mushrooms and onion; cook and stir 5-7 minutes or until tender and liquid is evaporated. Remove from pan; cool completely.
2. Drain beef; discard sauce or save for another use. Coarsely chop beef. In a small bowl, whisk egg and water.
3. Unfold one sheet of puff pastry. On a lightly floured surface, roll pastry into a 15x9-in. rectangle; cut crosswise into thirds, making three 5-in.-wide rectangles.
4. Place a cheese slice on one half of each rectangle; trim cheese to fit. Top each with a rounded tablespoon of mushroom mixture and 3 tablespoons beef. Brush edges of pastry with egg mixture. Fold pastry over filling; press edges with a fork to seal. Transfer to a parchment paper-lined baking sheet. Repeat with remaining pastry sheet and filling.
5. Brush tops with egg mixture. Bake 17-20 minutes or until golden brown.
FREEZE OPTION *Freeze unbaked pastries on a waxed paper-lined baking sheet until firm. Transfer to a resealable plastic freezer bag; return to freezer. To use, bake frozen pastries on a parchment paper-lined baking sheet in a preheated 400° oven for 20-25 minutes or until golden brown and heated through.*

PHYLLO-LAYERED PASTICHIO

FREEZE OPTION *Cool unbaked casseroles; cover and freeze. To use, partially thaw in the refrigerator overnight. Remove from refrigerator 30 minutes before baking. Preheat oven to 350°. Bake, uncovered, increasing time to 60-70 minutes or until golden brown and a thermometer inserted in center reads 165°.*

ENCHILADAS EL PASO

These have more of a spaghetti sauce-tomato taste than typical Southwestern dishes. I found this recipe many years ago and it quickly became a family favorite. It's even better when it is prepared one day and served the next.

—LORAINE MEYER BEND, OR

PREP: 20 MIN. • **BAKE:** 30 MIN.
MAKES: 10 SERVINGS

- 1 **pound lean ground beef (90% lean)**
- ½ **cup chopped onion**
- 1 **can (14½ ounces) diced tomatoes, drained**
- 1 **can (6 ounces) tomato paste**
- ½ **cup water**
- 3 **teaspoons chili powder**
- 1¼ **teaspoons salt**
- ¼ **teaspoon pepper**
- 10 **flour tortillas (8 inches), warmed**
- 2 **cups shredded cheddar cheese**

1. In a large skillet, cook beef and onion over medium heat until meat is no longer pink; drain. Stir in the tomatoes, tomato paste, water, chili powder, salt and pepper.

2. Spoon about ⅓ cup meat sauce down the center of each tortilla. Top each with 2 tablespoons cheese. Roll up and place seam side down in an ungreased 13x9-in. baking dish. Top with the remaining meat sauce and cheese.

3. Cover and refrigerate overnight, or cover and bake at 375° for 25 minutes. Uncover; bake 3-5 minutes longer or until heated through.

TO USE REFRIGERATED ENCHILADAS *Remove from the refrigerator 30 minutes before baking. Bake as directed.*

PHYLLO-LAYERED PASTICHIO

My grandfather always made pastichio on special occasions or when we had guests for dinner. I cherish the memories I have of him teaching me how to cook one of his signature dishes.

—TINA WAISMAN SAFETY HARBOR, FL

PREP: 1 HOUR • **BAKE:** 35 MIN. + STANDING
MAKES: 2 CASSEROLES (6 SERVINGS EACH)

- 1½ **pounds ground beef**
- 1 **medium onion, chopped**
- 1 **garlic clove, minced**
- 1 **can (15 ounces) tomato sauce**
- ¼ **cup white wine or beef broth**
- 1 **cinnamon stick (3 inches)**
- 1 **bay leaf**
- 1 **teaspoon sugar**
- ½ **teaspoon salt**
- ¼ **teaspoon pepper**

ASSEMBLY

- 1 **pound ziti or other small tube pasta**
- 1⅓ **cups grated Romano cheese**
- 4 **large eggs, lightly beaten**
- ¾ **cup butter, melted, divided**
- 20 **sheets phyllo dough (14x9 inches)**

1. Preheat oven to 350°. In a large skillet, cook beef, onion and garlic over medium heat 6-8 minutes or until meat is no longer pink, breaking up the beef into crumbles; drain.

2. Stir in tomato sauce, wine, cinnamon stick, bay leaf, sugar, salt and pepper. Bring to a boil; reduce heat and simmer 20-25 minutes or until thickened, stirring occasionally. Discard cinnamon stick and bay leaf.

3. Meanwhile, cook ziti according to package directions for al dente. Drain and return to pan. Stir in cheese, eggs and ¼ cup butter.

4. Place one sheet of phyllo dough on a work surface; brush with butter. Layer with nine additional phyllo sheets, brushing each layer. (Keep remaining phyllo covered with plastic wrap and a damp towel to prevent it from drying out.) Cut phyllo stack crosswise in half; place one stack in each of two greased 8-in. square baking dishes.

5. In each dish, layer 2 cups pasta mixture and 1 cup sauce. Repeat layers. Prepare a second stack of 10 phyllo sheets, brushing each with butter; cut stack in half and place one half-stack over each dish.

6. Bake, uncovered, 35-40 minutes or until golden brown. Let stand 15 minutes before cutting.

MUSHROOM BEEF

Top this hearty stew with crumbled blue cheese just before serving to add a burst of flavor. Serve some now and store the rest in the freezer for another meal.

—**NANCY LATULIPPE** SIMCOE, ON

PREP: 35 MIN. • **COOK:** 2 HOURS
MAKES: 9 SERVINGS

- 1 **carton (32 ounces) beef broth**
- 1 **ounce dried mixed mushrooms**
- ¼ **cup all-purpose flour**
- 1 **teaspoon salt**
- 1 **teaspoon pepper**
- 1 **boneless beef chuck roast (2 pounds), cubed**
- 3 **tablespoons canola oil**
- 1 **pound sliced baby portobello mushrooms**
- 5 **medium carrots, chopped**
- 1 **large onion, chopped**
- 3 **garlic cloves, minced**
- 3 **teaspoons minced fresh rosemary or 1 teaspoon dried rosemary, crushed**
- 2 **tablespoons cornstarch**
- 2 **tablespoons cold water**
  Hot cooked egg noodles, optional
- ¼ **cup crumbled blue cheese**

1. Bring beef broth and dried mushrooms to a boil in a large saucepan. Remove from heat; let stand 15-20 minutes or until mushrooms are softened. Drain mushrooms, reserving liquid; finely chop mushrooms. Set aside.

2. Combine flour, salt and pepper in a large resealable plastic bag; set aside 1 tablespoon for sauce. Add beef, a few pieces at a time, to the remaining flour mixture and shake to coat.

3. Brown beef in oil in batches in a Dutch oven. Add portobello mushrooms, carrots and onion; saute until the onion is tender. Add garlic, rosemary and rehydrated mushrooms; cook 1 minute. Stir in reserved flour mixture until blended; gradually add mushroom broth.

4. Bring to a boil. Reduce heat; cover and simmer 1½ to 2 hours or until beef is tender. Combine cornstarch and water until smooth; gradually stir into pan. Bring to a boil; cook and stir 2 minutes or until thickened. Serve with egg noodles if desired; top with blue cheese.

FREEZE OPTION *Freeze cooled stew in freezer containers up to 6 months. To use, thaw in the refrigerator overnight. Place in a Dutch oven; reheat. Serve with egg noodles if desired; top with blue cheese.*

POULTRY FAVORITES

Whether they're for casseroles, meatballs, potpies—
or served with rich sauces—great chicken and turkey
recipes squeeze delicious dinners into busy schedules!

FAVORITE CHICKEN POTPIE, P. 63

ITALIAN TURKEY SANDWICHES

Our family enjoys these tasty turkey sandwiches—it's a good thing the recipe makes plenty! This is a great dish for potlucks, and leftovers are just as good the next day.

—CAROL RILEY OSSIAN, IN

PREP: 10 MIN. • **COOK:** 5 HOURS
MAKES: 12 SERVINGS

- 1 bone-in turkey breast (6 pounds), skin removed
- 1 medium onion, chopped
- 1 small green pepper, chopped
- ¼ cup chili sauce
- 3 tablespoons white vinegar
- 2 tablespoons dried oregano or Italian seasoning
- 4 teaspoons beef bouillon granules
- 12 kaiser or hard rolls, split

1. Place turkey breast in a greased 5-qt. slow cooker. Add onion and green pepper.
2. Combine the chili sauce, vinegar, oregano and bouillon; pour over the turkey and vegetables. Cover and cook on low for 5-6 hours or until turkey is tender.
3. Shred the turkey with two forks and return to the slow cooker; heat through. Spoon ½ cup onto each roll.

FREEZE OPTION *Place the cooled meat and juice mixture in freezer containers. To use, partially thaw in refrigerator overnight. Microwave, covered, on high in a microwave-safe dish until heated through, gently stirring and adding a little water if necessary.*

THAI-STYLE CHICKEN

Because you add the chicken to the peppery marinade the night before, making dinner the following day couldn't be quicker!

—VICKI FLODEN STORY CITY, IA

PREP: 10 MIN. + MARINATING
BAKE: 20 MIN.
MAKES: 4 SERVINGS

- ¼ cup reduced-sodium soy sauce
- 3 tablespoons lemon juice
- 3 tablespoons coarsely chopped fresh basil or 1 tablespoon dried basil
- 2 tablespoons fat-free plain yogurt
- 2 teaspoons grated lemon peel
- 3 garlic cloves, minced
- 1 teaspoon ground ginger
- ½ to 1 teaspoon crushed red pepper flakes
- 4 boneless skinless chicken breast halves (4 ounces each)

1. In a small bowl, combine soy sauce, lemon juice, basil, yogurt, lemon peel, garlic, ginger and pepper flakes. Remove ¼ cup of the marinade to another bowl; cover and refrigerate. Pour the remaining marinade into a large resealable plastic bag; add the chicken. Seal bag and turn to coat; refrigerate overnight.
2. Drain and discard marinade from the bag. Place chicken in a 13 x 9-in. baking dish coated with cooking spray. Top with reserved marinade. Bake, uncovered, at 375° for 20 minutes or until a thermometer reads 170°.

ITALIAN TURKEY SANDWICHES

SPICY BEANS WITH TURKEY SAUSAGE

This jambalaya-type dish is a wonderful way to warm up cold winter nights. It works equally well for casual get-togethers or family dinners. For extra pizzazz, top each bowl with sour cream or shredded cheese.
—**DOROTHY JORDAN** COLLEGE STATION, TX

PREP: 25 MIN. • **COOK:** 5 HOURS
MAKES: 6 SERVINGS

- 1 **pound smoked turkey sausage, halved and sliced**
- 1 **can (16 ounces) kidney beans, rinsed and drained**
- 1 **can (15½ ounces) great northern beans, rinsed and drained**
- 1 **can (15 ounces) black beans, rinsed and drained**
- 1½ **cups frozen corn**
- 1½ **cups salsa**
- 1 **large green pepper, chopped**
- 1 **large onion, chopped**
- ½ **to 1 cup water**
- 3 **garlic cloves, minced**
- 1 **teaspoon ground cumin**

In a 5-qt. slow cooker, combine all ingredients. Cover and cook on low for 5-6 hours or until heated through. Stir before serving.
FREEZE OPTION *Freeze cooled stew in freezer containers. To use, partially thaw in refrigerator overnight. Heat through in a saucepan, stirring stew occasionally and adding a little water if necessary.*

✱

DID YOU KNOW? The reason for draining canned beans is to remove the excess salt used in the canning process. You may use the liquid in the can instead of adding water, but be sure to cut down or eliminate the water the recipe calls for, and adjust the salt level.

CHICKEN RANCH
MAC & CHEESE

CHICKEN RANCH MAC & CHEESE

Prep once, feed the family twice when you double this dish and freeze half. I created it for the people I love most, using ingredients they love best.
—**ANGELA SPENGLER** TAMPA, FL

PREP: 15 MIN. • **BAKE:** 30 MIN.
MAKES: 8 SERVINGS

- 3 **cups uncooked elbow macaroni**
- 3 **tablespoons butter**
- 2 **tablespoons all-purpose flour**
- ½ **teaspoon salt**
- ¼ **teaspoon pepper**
- 1 **cup 2% milk**
- 1½ **cups shredded cheddar cheese**
- ½ **cup grated Parmesan cheese**
- ½ **cup shredded Swiss cheese**
- ¾ **cup ranch salad dressing**
- 1 **cup coarsely chopped cooked chicken**

TOPPING
- ⅓ **cup seasoned bread crumbs**
- 2 **tablespoons butter, melted**
- 10 **bacon strips, cooked and crumbled**
- 1 **tablespoon minced fresh parsley**

1. Preheat oven to 350°. In a 6-qt. stockpot, cook macaroni according to package directions for al dente; drain and return to pot.
2. In a medium saucepan, melt butter over medium heat. Stir in flour, salt and pepper until smooth; gradually whisk in milk. Bring to a boil, stirring constantly; cook and stir 1-2 minutes or until thickened. Stir in the cheeses until blended. Stir in dressing.
3. Add the chicken and sauce to the macaroni; toss to combine. Transfer to a greased 13x9-in. baking dish.
4. Toss bread crumbs with melted butter; sprinkle over macaroni. Top with bacon. Bake, uncovered, 30-35 minutes or until topping is golden brown. Sprinkle with parsley.
FREEZE OPTION *Prepare recipe as directed, increasing milk to 1⅓ cups. Cool unbaked casserole; cover and freeze. To use, partially thaw in refrigerator overnight. Remove from refrigerator 30 minutes before baking. Preheat oven to 350°. Cover casserole with foil; bake 30 minutes. Uncover; continue baking as directed or until heated through and for a thermometer inserted in center to read 165°.*

TANGY TURKEY TOSTADAS

TANGY TURKEY TOSTADAS

My husband and I have busy schedules, so I often turn to this nutritious variation on fast-food tacos. They're so tasty and easy to make. I serve them with a tossed green salad and Spanish rice.

—JULIE HUNTINGTON MEMPHIS, TN

START TO FINISH: 25 MIN.
MAKES: 8 SERVINGS

- 1¼ pounds lean ground turkey
- ¾ cup sliced fresh mushrooms
- 1 medium green pepper, chopped
- 1 small onion, chopped
- 2 garlic cloves, minced
- 1 can (16 ounces) kidney beans, rinsed and drained
- 1 cup salsa
- 1 can (4 ounces) chopped green chilies
- 1 tablespoon chili powder
- 1 teaspoon ground cumin
- ½ teaspoon salt
- 4 drops hot pepper sauce
- 1½ cups reduced-fat Mexican cheese blend
- ½ cup frozen corn, thawed
- 16 tostada shells
- 2 cups shredded lettuce
- 1 cup chopped tomatoes
- ¼ cup minced fresh cilantro

1. In a large skillet, cook the turkey, mushrooms, pepper and onion over medium heat for 6-8 minutes or until turkey is no longer pink and the vegetables are tender, breaking turkey into crumbles; drain. Stir in garlic; cook 1 minute longer.

2. Stir in beans, salsa, green chilies, chili powder, cumin, salt and pepper sauce. Cook, uncovered, 4-5 minutes or until heated through. Add cheese and corn; heat through. Spread about ⅓ cup of the filling over each tostada shell. Sprinkle with lettuce, tomatoes and cilantro.

FREEZE OPTION *Freeze cooled meat mixture in freezer containers. To use, partially thaw in refrigerator overnight. Heat in a saucepan, stirring occasionally and adding a little water if necessary, until the meat mixture is heated through. Serve on tostada shells with toppings.*

CHIPOTLE-LIME CHICKEN THIGHS

CHIPOTLE-LIME CHICKEN THIGHS

Put leftovers from this delicious recipe to good use—use the chicken bones to make your own stock, and freeze the remaining chipotle peppers and sauce for a smoky Sunday chili.

—NANCY BROWN DAHINDA, IL

PREP: 15 MIN. + CHILLING • **GRILL:** 20 MIN.
MAKES: 4 SERVINGS

- 2 garlic cloves, peeled
- ¾ teaspoon salt
- 1 tablespoon lime juice
- 1 tablespoon minced chipotle pepper in adobo sauce
- 2 teaspoons adobo sauce
- 1 teaspoon chili powder
- 4 bone-in chicken thighs (about 1½ pounds)

1. Place garlic on a cutting board; sprinkle with salt. Using the flat side of a knife, mash garlic until it reaches a paste consistency; transfer garlic paste to a small bowl.
2. Stir in lime juice, pepper, adobo sauce and chili powder. Gently loosen skin from chicken thighs; rub garlic mixture under skin. Cover and refrigerate overnight.
3. Grill chicken, covered, on an oiled grill over medium-low heat for 20-25 minutes or until a thermometer reads 180°, turning once. If desired, remove and discard skin before serving.

SPICY SHREDDED CHICKEN

I love Mexican food, but not the high calorie count that often comes with it. This easy dish is delicious, a definite crowd-pleaser—and healthy! I serve the chicken with warm tortillas, rice, beans and salsa.
—HEATHER WALKER SCOTTSDALE, AZ

PREP: 40 MIN. • **COOK:** 4¼ HOURS
MAKES: 8 SERVINGS

- 2 tablespoons olive oil
- 1 pound boneless skinless chicken thighs
- 1 pound boneless skinless chicken breasts
- 3 cups reduced-sodium chicken broth, divided
- 6 green onions, chopped
- 1 medium green pepper, chopped
- 2 tablespoons ground cumin
- 1 tablespoon garlic powder
- 1 tablespoon chili powder
- 1 tablespoon paprika
- 1 teaspoon cayenne pepper
- ½ teaspoon salt
- ¼ teaspoon pepper
- 1 plum tomato, chopped

1. In a large skillet, heat oil over medium-high heat. Brown chicken in batches and transfer to a 3- or 4-qt. slow cooker. Add 1 cup broth to skillet and cook, stirring to loosen browned bits from pan. Add onions and green pepper; cook and stir 3-5 minutes or until the vegetables are tender. Stir in seasonings; cook 1-2 minutes. Add tomato and remaining broth; pour over chicken. Cook, covered, on low 4-5 hours or until chicken is tender.
2. Remove chicken from slow cooker. When cool enough to handle, shred meat with two forks; return to slow cooker. Cook, covered, on low for 15-20 minutes longer or until heated through. Serve with a slotted spoon.
FREEZE OPTION *Freeze cooled chicken mixture in freezer containers. To use, partially thaw in refrigerator overnight. Heat through in a saucepan, stirring occasionally and adding a little reduced-sodium broth or water if necessary.*

SPICY SHREDDED CHICKEN

CHICKEN THIGHS WITH SHALLOTS & SPINACH

What could be better than an entree that comes with its own creamy vegetable side? This dish makes an eye-catching presentation and goes together in no time flat for a healthy supper.

—GENNA JOHANNES WRIGHTSTOWN, WI

START TO FINISH: 30 MIN.
MAKES: 6 SERVINGS

- 6 **boneless skinless chicken thighs (about 1½ pounds)**
- ½ **teaspoon seasoned salt**
- ½ **teaspoon pepper**
- 1½ **teaspoons olive oil**
- 4 **shallots, thinly sliced**
- ⅓ **cup white wine or reduced-sodium chicken broth**
- 1 **package (10 ounces) fresh spinach, trimmed**
- ¼ **teaspoon salt**
- ¼ **cup fat-free sour cream**

1. Sprinkle chicken with seasoned salt and pepper. In a large nonstick skillet coated with cooking spray, heat oil over medium heat. Add chicken; cook 6 minutes on each side or until a thermometer reads 170°. Remove from pan; keep warm.

2. In the same pan, cook and stir the shallots until tender. Add wine; bring to a boil. Cook until wine is reduced by half. Add spinach and salt; cook and stir just until the spinach is wilted. Stir in sour cream; serve with chicken.

FREEZE OPTION *Before adding sour cream, cool chicken and spinach mixture. Freeze in freezer containers. To use, partially thaw in refrigerator overnight. Heat through slowly in a covered skillet until a thermometer inserted in chicken reads 165°, stirring occasionally. Stir in sour cream.*

CHICKEN THIGHS WITH SHALLOTS & SPINACH

BARBECUE SHEPHERD'S PIE

BARBECUE SHEPHERD'S PIE

Here's how to have a wholesome meal even on hectic nights! I add leftover veggies, such as green beans, sweet potatoes or corn, and zip it up with chipotle powder.

—ANGELA BUCHANAN LONGMONT, CO

PREP: 15 MIN. • **BAKE:** 30 MIN.
MAKES: 6 SERVINGS

- 1 **tablespoon olive oil**
- 1 **pound ground turkey**
- 1 **medium onion, chopped**
- 2 **medium carrots, thinly sliced**
- ½ **cup frozen peas**
- ½ **cup honey barbecue sauce**
- ⅓ **cup ketchup**
- 1 **package (24 ounces) refrigerated mashed potatoes**
- ½ **teaspoon paprika**

1. Preheat oven to 350°. In a large skillet, heat oil over medium heat. Add turkey and onion; cook 6-8 minutes or until the turkey is no longer pink, breaking up turkey into crumbles; drain. Stir in carrots, peas, barbecue sauce and ketchup.

2. Transfer mixture to a greased 1½-qt. baking dish. Spread mashed potatoes over top; sprinkle with paprika. Bake, uncovered, 30-35 minutes or until filling is bubbly.

FREEZE OPTION *Cool unbaked casserole; cover and freeze. To use, partially thaw in refrigerator overnight. Remove from refrigerator 30 minutes before baking. Preheat oven to 350°. Bake casserole as directed, increasing time as necessary to heat through and for a thermometer inserted in center to read 165°.*

LOADED CHICKEN & GOUDA CALZONES

When I had my daughter, I stocked the freezer with meals to make the first weeks easier. These calzones were one of our favorites! Because they freeze in individual portions, they also make a great lunch. Dip them in spaghetti sauce, pesto or ranch dressing—each is delicious!

—ELISABETH LARSEN PLEASANT GROVE, UT

PREP: 40 MIN. • **BAKE:** 15 MIN.
MAKES: 8 SERVINGS

- 1 tablespoon olive oil
- ½ pound sliced fresh mushrooms
- 1 small onion, finely chopped
- 2 garlic cloves, minced
- 1 package (10 ounces) frozen chopped spinach, thawed and squeezed dry
- 2 cups shredded cooked chicken breast
- 1 cup chopped roasted sweet red peppers, drained
- 6 bacon strips, cooked and crumbled
- ½ teaspoon salt
- ¼ teaspoon pepper
- 2 loaves (1 pound each) frozen whole wheat bread dough, thawed
- 2 cups shredded Gouda cheese
- 1 large egg white, lightly beaten

1. Preheat oven to 400°. In a large skillet, heat oil over medium-high heat. Add mushrooms and onion; cook and stir 3-5 minutes or until tender. Add garlic; cook 1 minute longer. Remove from heat. Stir in the spinach, chicken, red peppers, bacon, salt and pepper.

2. On a lightly floured surface, divide each loaf of dough into four portions; press or roll each into an 8-in. circle. Place ½ cup filling over half of each circle to within ½ in. of edge. Top each with ¼ cup cheese. Fold dough over filling; pinch edge to seal.

3. Place on greased baking sheets. Brush tops with egg white. Bake for 14-17 minutes or until golden brown and heated through. Serve warm.

FREEZE OPTION *Freeze cooled baked calzones in resealable plastic freezer bags. To use, place calzones on greased baking sheets. Cover with foil and reheat in a preheated 350° oven for 25 minutes. Uncover; bake for 5-10 minutes longer or until calzones are heated through.*

LOADED CHICKEN & GOUDA CALZONES

MEXICAN CHICKEN ALFREDO

MEXICAN CHICKEN ALFREDO

One family member likes Italian, another likes Mexican. They never have to argue when this rich and creamy sensation is on the menu!

—TIA WOODLEY STOCKBRIDGE, GA

PREP: 25 MIN. • **BAKE:** 30 MIN.
MAKES: 2 CASSEROLES (4 SERVINGS EACH)

- 1 package (16 ounces) gemelli or spiral pasta
- 2 pounds boneless skinless chicken breasts, cubed
- 1 medium onion, chopped
- ¼ teaspoon salt
- ¼ teaspoon pepper
- 1 tablespoon canola oil
- 2 jars (15 ounces each) Alfredo sauce
- 1 cup grated Parmesan cheese
- 1 cup medium salsa
- ¼ cup 2% milk
- 2 teaspoons taco seasoning

1. Preheat oven to 350°. Cook pasta according to package directions.

2. Meanwhile, in a large skillet over medium heat, cook chicken, onion, salt and pepper in oil until chicken is no longer pink. Stir in Alfredo sauce; bring to a boil. Stir in cheese, salsa, milk and taco seasoning.

3. Drain pasta; toss with chicken mixture. Divide between two greased 8-in. square baking dishes. Cover and bake 30-35 minutes or until bubbly.

FREEZE OPTION *Cover and freeze unbaked casserole up to 3 months. To use, thaw in refrigerator overnight. Remove from refrigerator 30 minutes before baking. Preheat oven to 350°. Bake casserole, covered, for 50-60 minutes or until bubbly.*

CHICKEN FLORENTINE MEATBALLS

JERK TURKEY TENDERLOINS

The salsa for these tenderloins is best when made with fresh pineapple; however, on particularly busy days, I've used canned pineapple tidbits to speed up the preparation.

—**HOLLY BAUER** WEST BEND, WI

START TO FINISH: 30 MIN.
MAKES: 5 SERVINGS (2 CUPS SALSA)

- 1 package (20 ounces) turkey breast tenderloins
- ½ teaspoon seasoned salt
- 2 tablespoons olive oil
- 1 tablespoon dried rosemary, crushed
- 1 tablespoon Caribbean jerk seasoning
- 1 tablespoon brown sugar

SALSA
- 1½ cups cubed fresh pineapple
- 1 medium sweet red pepper, chopped
- ¼ cup chopped red onion
- ¼ cup minced fresh cilantro
- 1 jalapeno pepper, seeded and minced
- 2 tablespoons lime juice
- 2 garlic cloves, minced
- ¼ teaspoon salt
- ⅛ teaspoon pepper

1. Sprinkle the turkey tenderloins with seasoned salt. Combine the oil, rosemary, jerk seasoning and brown sugar. Rub over the tenderloins. Broil 3-4 in. from the heat for 7-9 minutes on each side or until a thermometer reads 170°.

2. Meanwhile, in a bowl, combine the salsa ingredients. Serve with turkey.

FREEZE OPTION *Season turkey as directed. Transfer to a resealable plastic freezer bag; freeze. To use, completely thaw in refrigerator. Broil tenderloins and prepare salsa as directed.*

CHEAT IT! *Substitute a fruity deli salsa for the homemade salsa.*

NOTE *Wear disposable gloves when cutting hot peppers; the oils can burn skin. Avoid touching your face.*

CHICKEN FLORENTINE MEATBALLS

Served up over spaghetti squash in a mushroom-tomato sauce, these meatballs are tops.

—**DIANE NEMITZ** LUDINGTON, MI

PREP: 40 MIN. • **COOK:** 20 MIN.
MAKES: 6 SERVINGS

- 2 large eggs, lightly beaten
- 1 package (10 ounces) frozen chopped spinach, thawed and squeezed dry
- ½ cup dry bread crumbs
- ¼ cup grated Parmesan cheese
- 1 tablespoon dried minced onion
- 1 garlic clove, minced
- ¼ teaspoon salt
- ⅛ teaspoon pepper
- 1 pound ground chicken
- 1 medium spaghetti squash

SAUCE
- ½ pound sliced fresh mushrooms
- 2 teaspoons olive oil
- 1 can (14½ ounces) diced tomatoes, undrained
- 1 can (8 ounces) tomato sauce
- 2 tablespoons minced fresh parsley
- 1 garlic clove, minced
- 1 teaspoon dried oregano
- 1 teaspoon dried basil

1. In a large bowl, combine the first eight ingredients. Crumble chicken over the mixture and mix well. Shape into 1½-in. balls.

2. Place the meatballs on a rack in a shallow baking pan. Bake, uncovered, at 400° for 20-25 minutes or until no longer pink. Meanwhile, cut squash in half lengthwise; discard seeds. Place squash cut side down on a microwave-safe plate. Microwave, uncovered, on high for 15-18 minutes or until tender.

3. In a large nonstick skillet, saute mushrooms in oil until tender. Stir in remaining ingredients. Bring to a boil. Reduce heat; simmer, uncovered, 8-10 minutes or until slightly thickened. Add meatballs and heat through.

4. When the squash is cool enough to handle, use a fork to separate strands. Serve with meatballs and sauce.

FREEZE OPTION *Place individual portions of cooled meatballs and squash in freezer containers. To use, partially thaw in refrigerator overnight. Microwave, covered, on high in a microwave-safe dish until heated through, gently stirring and adding a little water if necessary.*

NOTE *This recipe was tested in a 1,100-watt microwave.*

(5) INGREDIENTS
PARMESAN CHICKEN NUGGETS

My 3-year-old went through a chicken-nuggets-and-French-fries-only stage, so I made these golden nuggets for him. Even the grown-ups liked them!
—AMANDA LIVESAY MOBILE, AL

START TO FINISH: 30 MIN.
MAKES: 8 SERVINGS

¼ cup butter, melted
1 cup panko (Japanese) bread crumbs
½ cup grated Parmesan cheese
½ teaspoon kosher salt
1½ pounds boneless skinless chicken breasts, cut into 1-inch cubes
Marinara sauce, optional

1. Place butter in a shallow bowl. Combine bread crumbs, cheese and salt in another shallow bowl. Dip chicken in butter, then roll in crumbs.
2. Place in a single layer on two 15x10x1-in. baking pans. Bake at 375° for 15-18 minutes or until no longer pink, turning once. If desired, serve with marinara sauce.
FREEZE OPTION *Cool the chicken nuggets. Freeze in freezer containers.*

To use, partially thaw in refrigerator overnight. Place on a baking sheet and reheat in a preheated 375° oven for 7-12 minutes or until heated through.
SPICY CHICKEN NUGGETS *Add ¼ to ½ teaspoon ground chipotle pepper to the bread crumb mixture.*
ITALIAN SEASONED CHICKEN NUGGETS *Add 2 teaspoons Italian seasoning to the bread crumb mixture.*
RANCH CHICKEN NUGGETS *Substitute crushed corn flakes for bread crumbs. Toss chicken cubes with ⅓ cup ranch salad dressing, then roll in corn flake mixture. Serve nuggets with additional ranch dressing.*

HONEY MUSTARD CHICKEN

Try different styles of mustard, such as Dijon, sweet-hot mustard or even Chinese—each will give your dish a different taste sensation. For spicier chicken, you can substitute cayenne pepper for some of the chili powder.
—RICHARD GALLOP PUEBLO, CO

PREP: 15 MIN. • **BAKE:** 45 MIN.
MAKES: 6 SERVINGS

½ cup honey
¼ cup prepared mustard

1 envelope ranch salad dressing mix
1 tablespoon dried parsley flakes
1½ teaspoons Italian seasoning
½ teaspoon dried basil
½ teaspoon chili powder
¼ teaspoon garlic powder
¼ teaspoon pepper
6 chicken drumsticks
6 bone-in chicken thighs

1. For sauce, in a small bowl, combine the first nine ingredients. Set aside ½ cup for serving. Place chicken in a greased 15x10x1-in. baking pan; drizzle with remaining sauce.
2. Bake, uncovered, at 350° for 45-50 minutes or until a thermometer reads 170°, basting occasionally with pan juices. Warm reserved sauce; serve with chicken.
FREEZE OPTION *Cool chicken. Freeze chicken with reserved sauce in freezer containers. To use, partially thaw in refrigerator overnight. Heat through slowly in a covered skillet until a thermometer inserted in chicken reads 165°, stirring occasionally and adding a little broth or water if necessary.*

JUST-LIKE-THANKSGIVING TURKEY MEAT LOAF

For a meal that makes any time of year a holiday, this tender turkey meat loaf is perfect. Complemented with a cranberry glaze, it's a mouthwatering dish.

—**MOLLIE BROWN** LOS ANGELES, CA

PREP: 30 MIN. + STANDING • **BAKE:** 45 MIN.
MAKES: 6 SERVINGS

- 1 cup seasoned stuffing cubes
- ½ cup milk
- 1 large egg, beaten
- 1 celery rib, finely chopped
- 1 small onion, grated
- 1 small carrot, grated
- ¼ cup dried cranberries
- ½ teaspoon salt
- ¼ teaspoon pepper
- 3 to 4½ teaspoons minced fresh sage
- 3 teaspoons minced fresh rosemary
- 1½ pounds lean ground turkey
- ½ cup whole-berry cranberry sauce
- ½ cup ketchup
- ⅛ teaspoon hot pepper sauce

1. Preheat oven to 375°. In a large bowl, combine stuffing cubes and milk. Let stand 10 minutes; break up stuffing cubes with a fork. Stir in egg, celery, onion, carrot, cranberries, salt and pepper. Combine sage and rosemary; add half to the mixture. Crumble turkey over mixture and mix well. Pat into an ungreased 9x5-in. loaf pan.

2. Bake, uncovered, for 25 minutes; drain if necessary. Combine cranberry sauce, ketchup, pepper sauce and remaining herbs; spread over meat loaf. Bake for 20-25 minutes or until no pink remains and a thermometer reads 165°.

FREEZE OPTION *Shape meat loaf in plastic wrap-lined loaf pan; cover and freeze until firm. Remove from pan and wrap securely in foil; return to freezer. To use, unwrap meat loaf and bake in pan as directed, increasing time as necessary for a thermometer inserted in center to read 165°.*

CASHEW CHICKEN CASSEROLE

I especially like this dish because I can get it ready the day before I need it. It's easy to whip up with common pantry items, including macaroni, canned soup and saltine crackers.

—**JULIE RIDLON** SOLWAY, MN

PREP: 15 MIN. • **BAKE:** 35 MIN.
MAKES: 6 SERVINGS

- 2 cups uncooked elbow macaroni
- 3 cups cubed cooked chicken
- ½ cup process cheese (Velveeta)
- 1 small onion, chopped
- ½ cup chopped celery
- ½ cup chopped green pepper
- 1 can (8 ounces) sliced water chestnuts, drained
- 1 can (10¾ ounces) condensed cream of mushroom soup, undiluted
- 1 can (10¾ ounces) condensed cream of chicken soup, undiluted
- 1⅓ cups milk
- 1 can (14½ ounces) chicken broth
- ¼ cup butter, melted
- ⅔ cup crushed saltines (about 20 crackers)
- ¾ cup cashew halves

1. In a greased 13x9-in. baking dish, layer the first seven ingredients in the order listed. In a large bowl, combine the soups, milk and broth. Pour over the water chestnuts. Cover casserole and refrigerate overnight.

2. Toss butter and cracker crumbs; sprinkle over casserole. Top with cashews. Bake, uncovered, at 350° for 35-40 minutes or until macaroni is tender.

CHICKEN MANICOTTI

When a girlfriend came home from the hospital with her newborn, I sent over this freezer casserole. She and her family raved over how good it was. Try swapping olives for the mushrooms or using veal instead of chicken.

—JAMIE VALOCCHI MESA, AZ

PREP: 25 MIN. • **BAKE:** 65 MIN.
MAKES: 2 CASSEROLES (4 SERVINGS EACH)

- 1 tablespoon garlic powder
- 1½ pounds boneless skinless chicken breasts
- 16 uncooked manicotti shells
- 2 jars (26 ounces each) spaghetti sauce, divided
- 1 pound bulk Italian sausage, cooked and drained
- ½ pound fresh mushrooms, sliced
- 4 cups (16 ounces) shredded part-skim mozzarella cheese
- ⅔ cup water

1. Preheat oven to 375°. Rub garlic powder over chicken; cut into 1-in. strips. Stuff chicken into manicotti shells. Spread 1 cup of the spaghetti sauce in each of two greased 13x9-in. baking dishes.
2. Place eight stuffed manicotti shells in each dish. Sprinkle with sausage and mushrooms. Pour remaining spaghetti sauce over the top. Sprinkle with cheese.
3. Drizzle water around the edge of each dish. Cover and bake 65-70 minutes or until chicken is no longer pink and the pasta is tender.
FREEZE OPTION *Cover and freeze unbaked casseroles for up to 1 month. To use, partially thaw in refrigerator overnight. Remove from refrigerator 30 minutes before baking. Preheat oven to 375°. Bake casseroles as directed, increasing time as necessary to heat through and for a thermometer inserted in center to read 165°.*

✳
DID YOU KNOW? You can freeze cranberries! Place them in a single layer on a 13x9-in. baking pan and freeze. Then transfer them to an airtight container and pop in the freezer; they'll keep for up to a year.

TART CRANBERRY CHICKEN

My husband loves chicken when it's nice and moist, like it is in this recipe. I serve it over hot fluffy rice with a salad and warm rolls. The tart, ruby-red sauce is also great for cooking pork chops.

—DOROTHY BATEMAN CARVER, MA

PREP: 20 MIN. • **COOK:** 20 MIN.
MAKES: 6 SERVINGS

- ½ cup all-purpose flour
- ½ teaspoon salt
- ¼ teaspoon pepper
- 6 boneless skinless chicken breast halves (4 ounces each)
- 3 tablespoons butter
- 1 cup water
- 1 cup fresh or frozen cranberries
- ½ cup packed brown sugar
  Dash ground nutmeg
- 1 tablespoon red wine vinegar, optional
  Hot cooked rice

1. In a shallow dish, combine flour, salt and pepper; dredge chicken in the flour mixture. In a skillet, melt butter over medium heat. Brown chicken on both sides. Remove and keep warm.
2. Add water, cranberries, brown sugar, nutmeg and, if desired, vinegar to the pan; cook and stir until the berries burst, about 5 minutes. Return chicken to skillet. Cover and simmer for 20-30 minutes or until the chicken is tender, basting occasionally with the sauce. Serve with rice.
FREEZE OPTION *Place chicken in freezer containers; top with sauce. If desired, place rice in separate freezer containers. Cool and freeze. To use, partially thaw in refrigerator overnight. Microwave, covered, on high in a microwave-safe dish until heated through, gently stirring and adding a little water if necessary.*

TART CRANBERRY CHICKEN

**POTATO CHIP
CHICKEN STRIPS**

POTATO CHIP CHICKEN STRIPS

This novel recipe makes a fast and tasty change from fried chicken.

—JUDITH LABROZZI CANTON, OH

PREP: 20 MIN. • **BAKE:** 20 MIN.
MAKES: 10 SERVINGS

- 1 **cup sour cream**
- ⅛ **teaspoon garlic salt**
- ⅛ **teaspoon onion salt**
- ⅛ **teaspoon paprika**
- 1 **package (12 ounces) potato chips, crushed**
- 2 **pounds boneless skinless chicken breasts, cut into 1-inch strips**
- ¼ **cup butter, melted**
   Salsa, barbecue sauce or sweet-and-sour sauce

1. In a shallow bowl, combine sour cream and seasonings. Place crushed potato chips in another shallow bowl. Dip chicken strips in sour cream mixture, then coat with potato chips. Place strips in a greased 15x10x1-in. baking pan. Drizzle with butter.
2. Bake at 400° for 20-22 minutes or until the chicken is no longer pink. Serve with salsa or sauce.
FREEZE OPTION *Transfer cooled chicken strips to a resealable plastic freezer bag; freeze. To use, reheat chicken strips in a greased 15x10x1-in. baking pan in a preheated 400° oven until crisp and heated through.*

FAVORITE CHICKEN POTPIE

Chock-full of chicken, potatoes and peas, this chilly-day favorite makes two golden pies, so you can serve one at dinner and save the other for a busy night.

—KAREN JOHNSON BAKERSFIELD, CA

PREP: 40 MIN. • **BAKE:** 35 MIN. + STANDING
MAKES: 2 POTPIES (8 SERVINGS EACH)

- 2 **cups diced peeled potatoes**
- 1¾ **cups sliced carrots**
- 1 **cup butter, cubed**
- ⅔ **cup chopped onion**
- 1 **cup all-purpose flour**
- 1¾ **teaspoons salt**
- 1 **teaspoon dried thyme**
- ¾ **teaspoon pepper**
- 3 **cups chicken broth**
- 1½ **cups milk**
- 4 **cups cubed cooked chicken**
- 1 **cup frozen peas**
- 1 **cup frozen corn**
- 2 **packages (14.1 ounces each) refrigerated pie pastry**

1. Preheat oven to 425°. Place potatoes and carrots in a large saucepan; add water to cover. Bring to a boil. Reduce heat; cook, covered, for 8-10 minutes or until vegetables are crisp-tender; drain.
2. In a large skillet, heat butter over medium-high heat. Add onion; cook and stir until tender. Stir in flour and seasonings until blended. Gradually stir in broth and milk. Bring to a boil, stirring constantly; cook and stir for 2 minutes or until thickened. Stir in the chicken, peas, corn and potato mixture; remove from heat.
3. Unroll a pie pastry sheet into each of two 9-in. pie plates; trim even with rims. Add chicken mixture. Unroll remaining pie pastry sheet; place over the filling. Trim, seal and flute the edges. Cut slits in tops.
4. Bake for 35-40 minutes or until crust is lightly browned. Let stand 15 minutes before cutting.
FREEZE OPTION *Cover and freeze unbaked pies. To use, remove from freezer 30 minutes before baking (do not thaw). Preheat oven to 425°. Place pies on baking sheets; cover edges loosely with foil. Bake for 30 minutes. Reduce oven setting to 350°; bake 70-80 minutes longer or until crust is golden brown and a thermometer inserted in center reads 165°.*

FAVORITE CHICKEN POTPIE

CHICKEN AND SWISS
STUFFING BAKE

CHICKEN CACCIATORE

This dish makes a good Sunday dinner because it's so simple to prepare. It's inexpensive as well. Best of all, it's loaded with vegetables.

—**BARBARA ROBERTS** COURTENAY, BC

PREP: 15 MIN. • **COOK:** 1½ HOURS
MAKES: 6 SERVINGS

- 1 broiler/fryer chicken (3½ to 4 pounds), cut up
- ¼ cup all-purpose flour
  Salt and pepper to taste
- 2 tablespoons olive oil
- 2 tablespoons butter
- 1 large onion, chopped
- 2 celery ribs, sliced
- 1 large green pepper, cut into strips
- ½ pound sliced fresh mushrooms
- 1 can (28 ounces) tomatoes, cut up and juice reserved
- 1 can (8 ounces) tomato sauce
- 1 can (6 ounces) tomato paste
- 1 cup dry red wine or water
- 1 teaspoon dried thyme
- 1 teaspoon dried rosemary, crushed
- 1 teaspoon dried oregano
- 1 teaspoon dried basil
- 3 garlic cloves, minced
- 1 tablespoon sugar
  Hot cooked pasta
  Grated Parmesan cheese

1. Dust chicken with flour. Season with salt and pepper. In a large skillet, brown chicken on all sides in oil and butter over medium-high heat. Remove chicken to platter.
2. In the same skillet, cook and stir onion, celery, pepper and mushrooms for 5 minutes. Stir in the tomatoes, tomato sauce, tomato paste, wine, herbs, garlic and sugar. Bring to a boil. Reduce heat; cover and simmer for 30 minutes.
3. Return chicken to skillet. Cover and simmer for 45-60 minutes or until the chicken is tender. Serve over pasta; sprinkle servings with Parmesan cheese.

CHICKEN AND SWISS STUFFING BAKE

I love to cook but just don't have much time. This casserole is both good and fast—which makes it my favorite kind of recipe! I serve it with a green salad.

—**JENA COFFEY** SUNSET HILLS, MO

PREP: 20 MIN. • **BAKE:** 25 MIN.
MAKES: 8 SERVINGS

- 1 can (10¾ ounces) condensed cream of mushroom soup, undiluted
- 1 cup milk
- 1 package (6 ounces) stuffing mix
- 2 cups cubed cooked chicken breast
- 2 cups fresh broccoli florets, cooked
- 2 celery ribs, finely chopped
- 1½ cups shredded Swiss cheese, divided

1. In a large bowl, combine soup and milk until blended. Add the stuffing mix with contents of the seasoning packet, chicken, broccoli, celery and 1 cup cheese. Transfer to a greased 13x9-in. baking dish.
2. Bake, uncovered, at 375° for 20 minutes or until heated through. Sprinkle with remaining cheese; bake 5 minutes longer or until the cheese is melted.
FREEZE OPTION *Sprinkle remaining cheese over unbaked casserole. Cover and freeze. To use, partially thaw in refrigerator overnight. Remove from refrigerator 30 minutes before baking. Preheat oven to 375°. Bake casserole as directed, increasing time as necessary to heat through and for a thermometer inserted in center to read 165°.*

SLOW COOKER

HERBED TURKEY BREASTS

An array of flavorful herbs enhances the tender, moist turkey breast in this comforting slow cooker dish.

—**LAURIE MACE** LOS OSOS, CA

PREP: 25 MIN. + MARINATING
COOK: 3½ HOURS
MAKES: 12 SERVINGS

- 1 can (14½ ounces) chicken broth
- ½ cup lemon juice
- ¼ cup packed brown sugar
- ¼ cup fresh sage
- ¼ cup fresh thyme leaves
- ¼ cup lime juice
- ¼ cup cider vinegar
- ¼ cup olive oil
- 1 envelope onion soup mix
- 2 tablespoons Dijon mustard
- 1 tablespoon minced fresh marjoram
- 1½ teaspoons paprika
- 1 teaspoon garlic powder
- 1 teaspoon pepper
- ½ teaspoon salt
- 2 boneless skinless turkey breast halves (2 pounds each)

1. In a blender, process the first 15 ingredients until blended. Pour marinade into a large resealable plastic bag; add the turkey. Seal the bag and turn to coat; refrigerate for 8 hours or overnight.

2. Transfer turkey and marinade to a 5-qt. slow cooker. Cover and cook on high for 3½-4½ hours or until a thermometer reads 165°.

FREEZE IT

To freeze the simple and classic **Chicken Cacciatore** (left), first let the chicken cool. Then freeze in freezer containers. To use, partially thaw in the refrigerator overnight. Heat through slowly in a covered skillet, stirring occasionally, until a thermometer reads 165°.

HERBED TURKEY BREASTS

PORK CLASSICS

Ham, sausage, bacon, chops, ribs or roast—there's seemingly no end to the ways pork adapts to bring joy to the dinner table. Choose a recipe and dive in; you're sure to find a new favorite dish!

MARINATED PORK CHOPS, P. 71

BARBECUE PORK AND PENNE SKILLET

I'm the proud mother of wonderful and active children. Simple, delicious and quick meals like this are perfect for us to enjoy together after errands, school activities and soccer practice are over.

—JUDY ARMSTRONG PRAIRIEVILLE, LA

START TO FINISH: 25 MIN.
MAKES: 8 SERVINGS

- 1 package (16 ounces) penne pasta
- 1 cup chopped sweet red pepper
- ¾ cup chopped onion
- 1 tablespoon butter
- 1 tablespoon olive oil
- 3 garlic cloves, minced
- 1 carton (16 ounces) fully cooked barbecued shredded pork
- 1 can (14½ ounces) diced tomatoes with mild green chilies, undrained
- ½ cup beef broth
- 1 teaspoon ground cumin
- 1 teaspoon pepper
- ¼ teaspoon salt
- 1¼ cups shredded cheddar cheese
- ¼ cup chopped green onions

1. Cook pasta according to package directions. Meanwhile, in a large skillet, saute red pepper and onion in butter and oil until tender. Add garlic; saute 1 minute longer. Stir in the pork, tomatoes, broth, cumin, pepper and salt; heat through.

2. Drain pasta. Add pasta and cheese to pork mixture; stir until blended. Sprinkle with green onions.

FREEZE IT

Freeze cooled pasta mixture in freezer containers. To use, partially thaw in refrigerator overnight. Place in a shallow microwave-safe dish. Cover and microwave on high until heated through.

BARBECUE PORK AND PENNE SKILLET

SLOW COOKER

SATAY-STYLE PORK STEW

Thai cuisine features flavors that are hot and sour, salty and sweet. This one-dish pork satay balances all those qualities with the right proportions of ginger and red pepper flakes, rice vinegar, garlic, lime juice and creamy peanut butter.

—NICOLE WERNER ANN ARBOR, MI

PREP: 25 MIN. • **COOK:** 8 HOURS
MAKES: 6 SERVINGS

- 1 boneless pork shoulder butt roast (3 to 4 pounds), cut into 1½-inch cubes
- 2 medium parsnips, peeled and sliced
- 1 small sweet red pepper, thinly sliced
- 1 cup chicken broth
- ¼ cup reduced-sodium teriyaki sauce
- 2 tablespoons rice vinegar
- 1 tablespoon minced fresh gingerroot
- 1 tablespoon honey
- 2 garlic cloves, minced
- ½ teaspoon crushed red pepper flakes
- ¼ cup creamy peanut butter
  Hot cooked rice, optional
- 2 green onions, chopped
- 2 tablespoons chopped dry roasted peanuts

In a 3-qt. slow cooker, combine the first 10 ingredients. Cover and cook on low for 8-10 hours or until pork is tender. Skim fat; stir in peanut butter. Serve with rice if desired; top with onions and peanuts.

FREEZE OPTION *Before adding toppings, freeze cooled stew in freezer containers. To use, partially thaw in refrigerator overnight. Heat through in a saucepan, stirring occasionally; add a little broth or water if necessary.*

CALGARY STAMPEDE RIBS

"More, please!" is what I hear whenever I serve these zippy, finger-licking ribs. The first time my husband and I tried them, we pronounced them the best ever. The recipe has its roots in the Calgary Stampede, an annual Western and agricultural fair and exhibition in our province.

—MARIAN MISIK SHERWOOD PARK, AB

PREP: 2½ HOURS + MARINATING
GRILL: 15 MIN. • **MAKES:** 8 SERVINGS

- 4 **pounds pork baby back ribs, cut into serving-size pieces**
- 3 **garlic cloves, minced**
- 1 **tablespoon sugar**
- 1 **tablespoon paprika**
- 2 **teaspoons each salt, pepper, chili powder and ground cumin**

BARBECUE SAUCE
- 1 **small onion, finely chopped**
- 2 **tablespoons butter**
- 1 **cup ketchup**
- ¼ **cup packed brown sugar**
- 3 **tablespoons lemon juice**
- 3 **tablespoons Worcestershire sauce**
- 2 **tablespoons cider vinegar**
- 1½ **teaspoons ground mustard**
- 1 **teaspoon celery seed**
- ⅛ **teaspoon cayenne pepper**

1. Rub ribs with garlic; place in a shallow roasting pan. Cover and bake at 325° for 2 hours. Cool slightly. Combine the seasonings and rub over ribs. Cover and refrigerate for 8 hours or overnight.

2. In a small saucepan, saute onion in butter until tender. Stir in the remaining ingredients. Bring to a boil. Reduce heat; cook and stir until thickened, about 10 minutes. Remove from the heat; set aside ¾ cup of sauce. Brush ribs with some of the remaining sauce.

3. Grill, covered, over medium heat for 12 minutes, turning and basting with sauce. Serve with reserved sauce.

✱
DID YOU KNOW? Before 1819, it was traditional Hawaiian practice for men and women to dine separately. This custom ended with a celebratory feast where King Kamahameha II ate with women—and the luau was born!

HAWAIIAN PORK ROAST

⑤ INGREDIENTS
HAWAIIAN PORK ROAST

Preparing a pork roast with bananas, liquid smoke and soy sauce produces a wonderfully tender meat with flavor that recalls the specialty I so enjoyed at Hawaiian luaus.

—MARY GAYLORD BALSAM LAKE, WI

PREP: 10 MIN. + MARINATING
BAKE: 4½ HOURS
MAKES: 8-10 SERVINGS

- 1 **boneless pork shoulder butt roast (3 to 4 pounds)**
- 4 **teaspoons liquid smoke**
- 4 **teaspoons soy sauce**
- 2 **unpeeled ripe bananas**
- ½ **cup water**

1. Place the roast on a 22x18-in. piece of heavy-duty foil; sprinkle with liquid smoke and soy sauce. Wash bananas and place them at the base of each side of roast. Pull sides of foil up around meat; add water. Seal foil tightly; wrap again with another piece of foil. Place in a shallow baking pan; refrigerate overnight, turning several times.

2. Place foil-wrapped meat in a roasting pan. Bake at 400° for 1 hour. Reduce heat to 325°; continue baking for 3½ hours. Drain; discard bananas and liquid. Shred meat with a fork.

FREEZE OPTION *Freeze cooled meat with some of the juices in freezer containers. To use, partially thaw in refrigerator overnight. Heat through in a saucepan, stirring occasionally and adding a little water if necessary.*

SAUSAGE, KALE & LENTIL STEW

I made a pot of this soup when I visited my sister and her family. Now I bring it along whenever I stop by, or I pack up a few containers for my nephew, who appreciates home-cooked meals while he's away at college!

—TIFFANY IHLE BRONX, NY

PREP: 20 MIN. • **COOK:** 45 MIN.
MAKES: 6 SERVINGS (2 QUARTS)

- 1 pound bulk pork sausage
- 10 baby carrots, chopped (about ¾ cup)
- 1 small onion, finely chopped
- 4 garlic cloves, minced
- 4 plum tomatoes, halved
- ¾ cup roasted sweet red peppers
- 1 cup dried lentils, rinsed
- 2 cans (14½ ounces each) vegetable broth
- 1 bay leaf
- ½ teaspoon ground cumin
- ¼ teaspoon pepper
- 2 cups coarsely chopped fresh kale

1. In a Dutch oven, cook sausage, carrots and onion over medium-high heat for 8-10 minutes or until sausage is no longer pink, breaking up the sausage into crumbles. Stir in garlic; cook 2 minutes longer. Drain.
2. Place tomatoes and red peppers in a food processor; process until finely chopped. Add to sausage mixture; stir in lentils, broth and seasonings. Bring to a boil. Reduce heat and simmer, covered, for 20 minutes, stirring occasionally.
3. Stir in kale; cook 10-15 minutes longer or until lentils and kale are tender. Remove bay leaf.
FREEZE OPTION *Freeze cooled stew in freezer containers. To use, partially thaw in refrigerator overnight. Heat through in a saucepan, stirring occasionally.*

SAUSAGE, KALE & LENTIL STEW

PORK AND GREEN CHILI CASSEROLE

I work at a local hospital and also part time for some area doctors, so I'm always on the lookout for good, quick recipes to fix for my family. Some of my co-workers and I often exchange recipes. This zippy casserole is one that was brought to a picnic at my house. People raved about it.

—DIANNE ESPOSITE NEW MIDDLETOWN, OH

PREP: 20 MIN. • **BAKE:** 30 MIN.
MAKES: 6 SERVINGS

- 1½ pounds boneless pork, cut into ½-inch cubes
- 1 tablespoon canola oil
- 1 can (15 ounces) black beans, rinsed and drained
- 1 can (10¾ ounces) condensed cream of chicken soup, undiluted
- 1 can (14½ ounces) diced tomatoes, undrained
- 2 cans (4 ounces each) chopped green chilies
- 1 cup quick-cooking brown rice
- ¼ cup water
- 2 to 3 tablespoons salsa
- 1 teaspoon ground cumin
- ½ cup shredded cheddar cheese

1. Preheat oven to 350°. In a large skillet, brown pork in oil; drain. Stir in the beans, soup, tomatoes, chilies, rice, water, salsa and cumin.
2. Pour into an ungreased 2-qt. baking dish. Bake, uncovered, for 30 minutes or until bubbly. Sprinkle with cheese; let stand 5 minutes before serving.
FREEZE OPTION *Sprinkle cheese over cooled unbaked casserole. Cover and freeze. To use, partially thaw in refrigerator overnight. Remove from refrigerator 30 minutes before baking. Preheat oven to 350°. Bake casserole as directed, increasing time as necessary to heat through and for a thermometer inserted into center to read 165°.*

ZESTY SAUSAGE & BEANS

Packed with sausage, beans and bacon, this hearty and delicious dish is guaranteed to satisfy even the largest of appetites.

—MELISSA JUST MINNEAPOLIS, MN

PREP: 30 MIN. • **COOK:** 5 HOURS
MAKES: 10 SERVINGS

- 2 pounds smoked kielbasa or Polish sausage, halved and sliced
- 2 cans (15 ounces each) black beans, rinsed and drained
- 1 can (15 ounces) great northern beans, rinsed and drained
- 1 can (15 ounces) thick and zesty tomato sauce
- 1 medium green pepper, chopped
- 1 medium onion, chopped
- 5 bacon strips, cooked and crumbled
- 3 tablespoons brown sugar
- 2 tablespoons cider vinegar
- 3 garlic cloves, minced
- ¼ teaspoon dried thyme
- ¼ teaspoon dried marjoram
- ¼ teaspoon cayenne pepper
  Hot cooked rice

In a large skillet, brown sausage. Transfer to a 4-qt. slow cooker; add beans, tomato sauce, green pepper, onion, bacon, brown sugar, vinegar, garlic, thyme, marjoram and cayenne. Cover and cook on low for 5-6 hours or until the vegetables are tender. Serve with rice.

FREEZE OPTION *Freeze cooled sausage and bean mixture in freezer containers. To use, partially thaw in refrigerator overnight. Heat through in a saucepan, stirring occasionally and adding a little broth or water if necessary.*

✱
TEST KITCHEN TIP You can snip the bottoms of thin, tender kale stems with a kitchen shears. But if the stems are thick, you'll want to remove them from the leaves completely. Place each leaf on a cutting board, fold the leaf in half lengthwise and use a knife to carefully slice away the stem.

MARINATED PORK CHOPS

MARINATED PORK CHOPS

I make these tasty grilled loin chops all the time, and my family never tires of them. The secret to the pork's tenderness is overnight marinating.

—JEAN NEITZEL BELOIT, WI

PREP: 5 MIN. + MARINATING
GRILL: 20 MIN.
MAKES: 6 SERVINGS

- ¾ cup canola oil
- ⅓ cup reduced-sodium soy sauce
- ¼ cup white vinegar
- 2 tablespoons Worcestershire sauce
- 1 tablespoon lemon juice
- 1 tablespoon prepared mustard
- 1 teaspoon salt
- 1 teaspoon pepper
- 1 teaspoon dried parsley flakes
- 1 garlic clove, minced
- 6 bone-in pork loin chops (1 inch thick and 8 ounces each)

1. In a large resealable plastic bag, combine the first 10 ingredients; add pork. Seal bag and turn to coat; refrigerate overnight.

2. Drain pork, discarding marinade. Grill, covered, over medium heat for 4-5 minutes on each side or until a thermometer reads 145°. Let meat stand for 5 minutes before serving.

FREEZE OPTION *Freeze uncooked pork in bag with marinade. To use, completely thaw in refrigerator. Grill as directed.*

JIFFY GROUND PORK SKILLET

Some people call it dinner hour, but many of us call it rush hour! Slow down with this super-easy meal. The only thing you'll have left over is time to share with your family at the table.

—**BRIGITTE SCHALLER** FLEMINGTON, MO

START TO FINISH: 30 MIN.
MAKES: 5 SERVINGS

- 1½ cups uncooked penne pasta
- 1 pound ground pork
- ½ cup chopped onion
- 1 can (14½ ounces) stewed tomatoes, undrained
- 1 can (8 ounces) tomato sauce
- 1 teaspoon Italian seasoning
- 1 medium zucchini, cut into ¼-inch slices

1. Cook pasta according to the package directions. Meanwhile, in a large skillet, cook pork and onion over medium heat until meat is no longer pink; drain. Add tomatoes, tomato sauce and Italian seasoning. Bring to a boil. Reduce heat; cover and cook for 5 minutes to allow flavors to blend.
2. Drain pasta; add to skillet. Stir in zucchini. Cover and cook for 3-5 minutes or until the zucchini is crisp-tender.

FREEZE OPTION *Transfer individual portions of cooled pasta mixture to freezer containers. To use, partially thaw in refrigerator overnight. Heat through in a saucepan, stirring occasionally and adding a little tomato sauce if necessary.*

JIFFY GROUND PORK SKILLET

SLOW COOKER 🍲
LOW & SLOW PORK VERDE

My family loves this versatile pork dish. We usually have it over a serving of cheesy grits, but it also goes well with rice or potatoes. Leftovers make an excellent starter for white chili.

—**VAL RUBLE** AVA, MO

PREP: 15 MIN. • **COOK:** 5 HOURS
MAKES: 8 SERVINGS

- 1 boneless pork shoulder butt roast (3½ to 4 pounds)
- 1 large onion, chopped
- 1 jar (16 ounces) salsa verde
- 2 cans (4 ounces each) chopped green chilies
- 2 teaspoons ground cumin
- 1 teaspoon dried oregano
- 1 teaspoon salt
- 1 teaspoon pepper
- ¼ teaspoon crushed red pepper flakes
- ⅛ teaspoon ground cinnamon
- ¼ cup minced fresh cilantro
  Hot cooked grits
  Sour cream, optional

1. Place pork and onion in a 4-qt. slow cooker. In a small bowl, combine salsa, chilies, cumin, oregano, salt, pepper, pepper flakes and cinnamon; pour over meat. Cook, covered, on low for 5-6 hours or until the meat is tender.
2. Remove roast; cool slightly. Skim fat from cooking juices. Shred pork with two forks. Return meat to slow cooker; heat through. Stir in cilantro. Serve with grits and, if desired, sour cream.

FREEZE OPTION *Freeze cooled meat mixture in freezer containers. To use, partially thaw in refrigerator overnight. Microwave, covered, on high in a microwave-safe dish until heated through, gently stirring and adding a little broth if necessary.*

GRILLED PORK TENDERLOINS

We do a lot of grilling during the summer months, and this recipe is one my family asks for again and again.

—**BETSY CARRINGTON** LAWRENCEBURG, TN

PREP: 10 MIN. + MARINATING
GRILL: 20 MIN.
MAKES: 8 SERVINGS

- ⅓ cup honey
- ⅓ cup reduced-sodium soy sauce
- ⅓ cup teriyaki sauce
- 3 tablespoons brown sugar
- 1 tablespoon minced fresh gingerroot
- 3 garlic cloves, minced
- 4 teaspoons ketchup
- ½ teaspoon onion powder
- ½ teaspoon ground cinnamon
- ¼ teaspoon cayenne pepper
- 2 pork tenderloins (about 1 pound each)
  Hot cooked rice

1. In a large bowl, combine the first 10 ingredients. Pour half the marinade into a large resealable plastic bag; add tenderloins. Seal bag and turn to coat; refrigerate 8 hours or overnight, turning occasionally. Cover and refrigerate remaining marinade.

2. Drain and discard marinade from meat. Grill, covered, over indirect medium-hot heat for 20-35 minutes or until a thermometer reads 145°, turning occasionally and basting with reserved marinade. Let stand 5 minutes before slicing. Serve with rice.

FREEZE OPTION *Freeze uncooked pork in bag with half the marinade; freeze the reserved marinade in an individual freezer container. To use, completely thaw tenderloins and marinade in refrigerator. Grill as directed.*

GRILLED PORK TENDERLOINS

FREEZE IT

Freeze cooled pork mixture in freezer containers. To use, partially thaw in refrigerator overnight. Microwave, covered, on high in a microwave-safe dish until heated through, gently stirring and adding a little broth or water if necessary.

MEXICAN PORK & PINTO BEANS

MEXICAN PORK & PINTO BEANS

We've lived in Arizona for decades, and to us, Arizona-style cooking means Mexican-style cooking—and vice versa. Nothing tastes better than chili-spiced pork with tortillas.

—ANNE FATOUT PHOENIX, AZ

PREP: 30 MIN. • **COOK:** 4 HOURS
MAKES: 16 SERVINGS (4 QUARTS)

- 1 bone-in pork loin roast (3 pounds), trimmed
- 1 package (16 ounces) dried pinto beans, soaked overnight
- 4 to 5 cloves garlic, minced
- 2 tablespoons chili powder
- 1 to 1½ teaspoons ground cumin
- 1 teaspoon dried oregano
- 2 cans (4 ounces each) chopped green chilies
  Pepper to taste
- 5 medium carrots, sliced
- 4 celery ribs, sliced
- 1 can (14½ ounces) diced tomatoes, undrained
- 3 small zucchini, sliced
  Flour tortillas, warmed

1. In a stockpot, combine the first eight ingredients; cover with water. Bring to a boil. Reduce heat; simmer, covered, 3-4 hours or until meat and beans are tender.

2. Remove pork; cool slightly. Stir carrots, celery and tomatoes into bean mixture; return to a boil. Reduce heat; simmer, covered, until vegetables are crisp-tender. Add zucchini; cook for 8-10 minutes longer or until crisp-tender.

3. Meanwhile, remove pork from bone; discard bone. Cut pork into bite-size pieces; return to pot and heat through. Serve with tortillas.

FRENCH CANADIAN TOURTIERES

This recipe comes from my big sister. Each fall, we get together and make about 20 of these pies to use at Christmas, give as gifts or freeze in case of unexpected company.

—PAT MENEE CARBERRY, MB

PREP: 45 MIN. • **BAKE:** 40 MIN.
MAKES: 4 PIES (8 SERVINGS EACH)

- 4 celery ribs
- 4 medium carrots
- 2 large onions
- 2 garlic cloves, peeled
- 4 pounds ground pork
- 2 pounds ground veal
- 2 pounds bulk pork sausage
- 1 can (14½ ounces) chicken broth
- ½ cup minced fresh parsley
- 1 tablespoon salt
- 1 teaspoon pepper
- 1 teaspoon dried basil
- 1 teaspoon dried rosemary, crushed
- 1 teaspoon cayenne pepper
- 1 teaspoon ground mace
- 1 teaspoon ground cloves
- 1 cup dry bread crumbs
  Pastry for four double-crust pies (9 inches)

1. Coarsely chop celery, carrots and onions; place in a food processor with garlic. Cover and process until finely chopped; set aside.

2. In a stockpot or two Dutch ovens, cook vegetables, pork, veal and sausage until meat is no longer pink; drain. Stir in broth, parsley and seasonings. Reduce heat; cover and cook on low for 20 minutes. Stir in bread crumbs.

3. Preheat oven to 400°. Line four 9-in. pie plates with bottom crusts; trim pastry even with edges. Fill each with about 4 cups filling. Roll out remaining pastry to fit tops of pies; place over filling. Trim, seal and flute edges. Cut slits in pastry.

4. Cover edges of pies loosely with foil. Bake for 25 minutes. Reduce heat to 350°; remove foil and bake 15-20 minutes longer or until crusts are golden brown.

FREEZE OPTION *Cover and freeze unbaked pies. To use a pie, remove from freezer 30 minutes before baking (do not thaw). Preheat oven to 400°. Place pie on a baking sheet; cover edge loosely with foil. Bake for 25 minutes. Reduce heat to 350°. Remove foil and bake 50-60 minutes longer or until crust is golden brown and a thermometer inserted into center reads 165°.*

FRENCH CANADIAN TOURTIERES

PORK, BEAN &
RICE BURRITOS

discard remaining juices. Shred pork with two forks. Return meat and reserved juices to slow cooker; heat through.

3. Spoon a scant ⅓ cup shredded pork across center of each tortilla; top with a scant ⅓ cup each beans and rice. Fold bottom and sides of tortilla over filling and roll up. Serve with toppings as desired.

FREEZE OPTION *Cool filling ingredients before making burritos. Individually wrap burritos in paper towels and foil; freeze in a resealable plastic freezer bag. To use, remove foil; place paper towel-wrapped burrito on a microwave-safe plate. Microwave on high for 3-4 minutes or until heated through, turning once. Let stand 20 seconds.*

BRUNCH ENCHILADAS

I was looking for a healthier alternative to a favorite brunch casserole, and came up with this. The enchiladas are hearty, delicious and fun, and I really like that I can make them the day before!

—**GAIL SYKORA** MENOMONEE FALLS, WI

PREP: 15 MIN. + CHILLING
BAKE: 40 MIN. + STANDING
MAKES: 10 SERVINGS

- 2 cups cubed fully cooked ham
- ½ cup chopped green onions
- 10 fat-free flour tortillas (8 inches)
- 2 cups shredded reduced-fat cheddar cheese
- 1 tablespoon all-purpose flour
- 2 cups fat-free milk
- 1½ cups egg substitute

1. Combine ham and onions; place ⅓ cup down the center of each tortilla. Top with 2 tablespoons cheese. Roll up; place seam side down in a greased 13x9-in. baking dish.
2. In a large bowl, whisk flour, milk and egg substitute until smooth. Pour over tortillas. Cover and refrigerate for 8 hours or overnight.
3. Remove from the refrigerator 30 minutes before baking. Cover and bake at 350° for 25 minutes. Uncover; bake 10 minutes longer. Sprinkle with remaining cheese; bake for 3 minutes or until the cheese is melted. Let stand for 10 minutes before serving.

SLOW COOKER

PORK, BEAN &
RICE BURRITOS

The combination of spices is key to this delicious slow-cooked pork—it's my family's favorite burrito filling. The aroma that fills the air as the pork slowly simmers reminds me of a Mexican restaurant!

—**VALONDA SEWARD** COARSEGOLD, CA

PREP: 25 MIN. • **COOK:** 6 HOURS
MAKES: 10 SERVINGS

SPICE RUB

- 2½ teaspoons garlic powder
- 2 teaspoons onion powder
- 1¼ teaspoons salt
- 1 teaspoon white pepper
- 1 teaspoon pepper
- ½ teaspoon ground cumin
- ½ teaspoon dried oregano
- ½ teaspoon cayenne pepper

BURRITOS

- 1 boneless pork shoulder butt roast (3 pounds)
- 1 cup water
- 2 tablespoons beef bouillon granules
- 10 flour tortillas (10 inches)
- 3 cups canned pinto beans, rinsed and drained
- 3 cups cooked Spanish rice
  Optional toppings: salsa, chopped tomato, shredded lettuce, sour cream and guacamole

1. Mix spice rub ingredients; rub over pork. Transfer to a 6-qt. slow cooker. In a small bowl, mix water and beef granules; pour around the roast. Cook, covered, on low 6-8 hours or until the meat is tender.
2. Remove the roast; cool slightly. Reserve ½ cup of the cooking juices;

VEGGIE NOODLE HAM CASSEROLE

This saucy main dish is really versatile. Without the ham, it can be a vegetarian entree or a hearty side dish.

—**JUDY MOODY** WHEATLEY, ON

PREP: 15 MIN. • **BAKE:** 50 MIN.
MAKES: 8-10 SERVINGS

- 1 package (12 ounces) wide egg noodles
- 1 can (10¾ ounces) condensed cream of chicken soup, undiluted
- 1 can (10¾ ounces) condensed cream of broccoli soup, undiluted
- 1½ cups milk
- 2 cups frozen corn, thawed
- 1½ cups frozen California-blend vegetables, thawed
- 1½ cups cubed fully cooked ham
- 2 tablespoons minced fresh parsley
- ½ teaspoon pepper
- ¼ teaspoon salt
- 1 cup shredded cheddar cheese, divided

1. Preheat oven to 350°. Cook pasta according to package directions; drain. In a large bowl, combine soups and milk; stir in the noodles, corn, vegetables, ham, parsley, pepper, salt and ¾ cup of cheese.
2. Transfer to a greased 13x9-in. baking dish. Cover and bake for 45 minutes. Uncover; sprinkle with remaining cheese. Bake 5-10 minutes or until bubbly and cheese is melted.
FREEZE OPTION *Cool unbaked casserole; cover and freeze. To use, partially thaw in refrigerator overnight. Remove from refrigerator 30 minutes before baking. Preheat oven to 350°. Bake casserole as directed, increasing time as necessary to heat through and for a thermometer inserted in center to read 165°. Top with remaining cheese for the last 5 minutes.*

BBQ COUNTRY RIBS

I created my sauce for ribs many years ago by adapting a recipe I saw in a magazine. I often triple the sauce and keep some in my freezer to use on chicken, beef or pork.

—**BARBARA GERRIETS** TOPEKA, KS

PREP: 25 MIN. • **BAKE:** 2 HOURS
MAKES: 8 SERVINGS

- 2½ pounds boneless country-style pork ribs
- 2 teaspoons liquid smoke, optional
- ½ teaspoon salt
- 1 cup water

BARBECUE SAUCE
- ⅔ cup chopped onion
- 1 tablespoon canola oil
- ¾ cup each water and ketchup
- ⅓ cup lemon juice
- 3 tablespoons sugar
- 3 tablespoons Worcestershire sauce
- 2 tablespoons prepared mustard
- ½ teaspoon salt
- ½ teaspoon pepper
- ¼ teaspoon liquid smoke, optional

1. Place ribs in an 11x7-in. baking dish coated with cooking spray. Sprinkle with liquid smoke if desired and salt. Add water to pan. Cover and bake at 350° for 1 hour.
2. Meanwhile, in a saucepan, saute onion in oil until tender. Add the remaining sauce ingredients; bring to a boil. Reduce heat; simmer, uncovered, for 15 minutes or until slightly thickened.
3. Drain ribs; top with half of the barbecue sauce. Cover and bake 1 hour longer or until meat is tender, basting every 20 minutes. Serve with the remaining sauce.
FREEZE OPTION *Place cooled meat mixture in freezer containers. To use, partially thaw in refrigerator overnight. Microwave, covered, on high in a microwave-safe dish until heated through, gently stirring and adding a little water if necessary.*

BBQ COUNTRY RIBS

BACON TORTELLINI BAKE

COMPANY LASAGNA

I love having this in the fridge when guests come over. It's so easy, I can focus on socializing, not stress about dinner.

—**RENEE VAUGHAN** GALENA, OH

PREP: 40 MIN. + CHILLING
BAKE: 50 MIN. + STANDING
MAKES: 12 SERVINGS

- 1 pound bulk pork sausage
- 2 cans (one 28 ounces, one 14½ ounces) stewed tomatoes, undrained
- 1 can (6 ounces) tomato paste
- 2 tablespoons dried oregano
- 4 garlic cloves, minced
- ¼ teaspoon salt
- ¼ teaspoon pepper
- 4 cups shredded part-skim mozzarella cheese, divided
- 3 cups 2% cottage cheese
- 1 cup grated Parmesan cheese
- 2 large eggs, lightly beaten
- 3 tablespoons dried parsley flakes
- 12 no-cook lasagna noodles

1. In a Dutch oven, cook sausage over medium heat until no longer pink; drain. Stir in the tomatoes, tomato paste, oregano, garlic, salt and pepper. Bring to a boil. Reduce heat; simmer, uncovered, for 15-20 minutes or until thickened.
2. Meanwhile, in a large bowl, combine 2 cups mozzarella cheese, cottage cheese, Parmesan cheese, eggs and parsley.
3. Spread 1 cup meat mixture into a greased 13x9-in. baking dish. Layer with three noodles, 1¼ cups meat mixture and 1 cup cheese mixture. Repeat three times. Top with the remaining mozzarella cheese. Cover and refrigerate for 8 hours or overnight.
4. Remove from the refrigerator 30 minutes before baking. Cover and bake at 350° for 30 minutes. Uncover and bake 20-25 minutes longer or until bubbly and cheese is melted. Let stand for 10 minutes before cutting.

BACON TORTELLINI BAKE

I whipped up an easy pasta dish one night and it turned out to be a huge hit with my family. Broccoli and bacon add fabulous crunch to the creamy tortellini.

—**AMY LENTS** GRAND FORKS, ND

PREP: 25 MIN. • **BAKE:** 15 MIN.
MAKES: 6 SERVINGS

- 1 package (20 ounces) refrigerated cheese tortellini
- 3 cups small fresh broccoli florets
- ½ pound bacon strips, cut into 1-inch pieces
- 2 garlic cloves, minced
- 1 tablespoon all-purpose flour
- 1 teaspoon dried basil
- ½ teaspoon salt
- ⅛ teaspoon coarsely ground pepper
- 2 cups 2% milk
- ¾ cup shredded part-skim mozzarella cheese, divided
- ¾ cup grated Parmesan cheese, divided
- 2 teaspoons lemon juice

1. Preheat oven to 350°. Cook tortellini according to package directions, adding broccoli during the last 2 minutes; drain.
2. Meanwhile, in a large skillet, cook bacon over medium heat until crisp, stirring occasionally. Remove with a slotted spoon; drain on paper towels. Discard most of the drippings, reserving 1 tablespoon in pan.
3. Reduce heat to medium-low. Add garlic to the drippings in pan; cook and stir 1 minute. Stir in flour, basil, salt and pepper until blended; gradually whisk in milk. Bring to a boil, stirring constantly; cook and stir 3-5 minutes or until slightly thickened. Remove from heat.
4. Stir in ½ cup mozzarella cheese, ½ cup Parmesan cheese and lemon juice. Add tortellini mixture and bacon; toss to combine. Transfer to a greased 13x9-in. baking dish; sprinkle with remaining cheeses. Bake, uncovered, 15-20 minutes or until heated through and broccoli is tender.
FREEZE OPTION *Sprinkle remaining cheeses over unbaked casserole. Cover and freeze. To use, partially thaw in refrigerator overnight. Remove from refrigerator 30 minutes before baking. Preheat oven to 350°. Bake casserole as directed, increasing time as necessary to heat through and for a thermometer inserted in center to read 165°.*

HAM & COLLARDS QUICHE

HAM & COLLARDS QUICHE

I love quiche and wanted to make something that incorporates my Southern roots, so I came up with this version. With eggs, cheese, ham and nutritious collard greens in a flaky crust, it's a complete meal.
—**BILLIE WILLIAMS-HENDERSON** BOWIE, MD

PREP: 20 MIN. • **BAKE:** 35 MIN. + STANDING
MAKES: 6 SERVINGS

- 1 **sheet refrigerated pie pastry**
- 2 **cups shredded Colby-Monterey Jack cheese, divided**
- ¾ **cup cubed fully cooked ham**
- 2 **tablespoons olive oil**
- 1 **cup frozen chopped collard greens, thawed and drained**
- 1 **small onion, chopped**
- 1 **garlic clove, minced**
- ¼ **teaspoon salt**
- ¼ **teaspoon pepper**
- 6 **large eggs**
- 1 **cup 2% milk**

1. Preheat oven to 375°. Unroll pastry sheet into a 9-in. pie plate; flute edge. Sprinkle 1 cup cheese onto the bottom of the pastry-lined pie plate. Sprinkle with ham.

2. In a large skillet, heat oil over medium-high heat. Add the collard greens and onion; cook and stir for 5-7 minutes or until onion is tender. Add garlic; cook 1 minute longer. Stir in salt and pepper. Arrange the greens over the ham.

3. In a large bowl, whisk eggs and milk until blended. Pour over top. Sprinkle with remaining cheese.

4. Bake on lower oven rack for 35-40 minutes or until a knife inserted near center comes out clean. Let stand 10 minutes before cutting.
FREEZE OPTION *Cover and freeze unbaked quiche. To use, remove from freezer 30 minutes before baking (do not thaw). Preheat oven to 375°. Place quiche on a baking sheet. Bake as directed, increasing time to 50-60 minutes.*

✱
TEST KITCHEN TIP Collard greens, a member of the cabbage family, are becoming more popular, but still can be hard to find in some regions. If you need a substitute, try mustard greens, kale or bok choy.

PEPPERONI STROMBOLI

PEPPERONI STROMBOLI

Because this savory stromboli relies on frozen bread dough, it comes together in no time. The golden loaf is stuffed with cheese, pepperoni, mushrooms, peppers and olives. I often add a few thin slices of ham, too. It's tasty served with warm pizza sauce for dipping.

—**JENNY BROWN** WEST LAFAYETTE, IN

PREP: 20 MIN. • **BAKE:** 35 MIN.
MAKES: 10-12 SLICES

- 1 loaf (1 pound) frozen bread dough, thawed
- 2 large eggs, separated
- 1 tablespoon grated Parmesan cheese
- 1 tablespoon olive oil
- 1 teaspoon minced fresh parsley
- 1 teaspoon dried oregano
- ½ teaspoon garlic powder
- ¼ teaspoon pepper
- 8 ounces sliced pepperoni
- 2 cups shredded part-skim mozzarella cheese
- 1 can (4 ounces) mushroom stems and pieces, drained
- ¼ to ½ cup pickled pepper rings
- 1 medium green pepper, diced
- 1 can (2¼ ounces) sliced ripe olives
- 1 can (15 ounces) pizza sauce

1. Preheat oven to 350°. On a greased baking sheet, roll out dough into a 15x10-in. rectangle. In a small bowl, combine egg yolks, Parmesan cheese, oil, parsley, oregano, garlic powder and pepper. Brush over the dough.
2. Sprinkle with pepperoni, cheese, mushrooms, pepper rings, green pepper and olives. Roll up jelly-roll style, starting with a long side; pinch seam to seal and tuck ends under.
3. Place seam side down; brush top with egg whites. Do not let rise. Bake 35-40 minutes or until golden brown. Warm the pizza sauce; serve with sliced loaf.
FREEZE OPTION *Freeze cooled, unsliced pizza loaf in heavy-duty foil. To use, remove from freezer 30 minutes before reheating. Remove loaf from foil and reheat on a greased baking sheet in a preheated 325° oven until heated through. Serve as directed.*

CREAMY NOODLE CASSEROLE

CREAMY NOODLE CASSEROLE

My husband works long hours and frequently won't arrive home until after 7 o'clock. But this casserole is still tasty after it's been warmed in the microwave!

—**BARB MARSHALL** PICKERINGTON, OH

START TO FINISH: 25 MIN.
MAKES: 8 SERVINGS

- 1 package (12 ounces) egg noodles
- 1 package (16 ounces) frozen broccoli cuts
- 3 cups cubed fully cooked ham
- 1 cup shredded part-skim mozzarella cheese
- 1 cup shredded Parmesan cheese
- ⅓ cup butter, cubed
- ½ cup half-and-half cream
- ¼ teaspoon each garlic powder, salt and pepper

1. In a Dutch oven, cook noodles in boiling water for 5 minutes. Add broccoli and ham; cook 5-10 minutes longer or until noodles are tender.
2. Drain; return to pan. Stir in the remaining ingredients. Cook and stir over low heat until butter is melted and mixture is heated through.
FREEZE OPTION *Freeze cooled noodle mixture in freezer containers. To use, partially thaw in refrigerator overnight. Microwave, covered, on high in a microwave-safe dish until heated through, gently stirring and adding a little broth or milk if necessary.*

GREAT NORTHERN BEAN STEW

This hearty, delicious stew comes together quickly and cooks in an hour. It freezes well, too!

—**MILDRED SHERRER** FORT WORTH, TX

PREP: 20 MIN. • **COOK:** 55 MIN.
MAKES: 6 SERVINGS

- 1 pound bulk pork sausage
- 1 cup chopped onion
- 1 can (15½ ounces) great northern beans, rinsed and drained
- 1 can (28 ounces) diced tomatoes, undrained
- 2 cups chopped cabbage
- 1 cup sliced carrots
- 1 tablespoon white vinegar
- 1 tablespoon brown sugar
- ½ teaspoon salt
- ½ teaspoon dried thyme
- ½ teaspoon paprika
- ½ teaspoon pepper
- ¼ teaspoon hot pepper sauce
- 2 tablespoons minced fresh parsley

1. In a large saucepan, cook sausage and onion over medium heat until meat is no longer pink; drain. Add the next 11 ingredients. Bring to a boil. Reduce heat; simmer, covered, for 50-60 minutes or until vegetables are tender.
2. Stir in parsley; cook 5 minutes longer.
FREEZE OPTION *Freeze cooled stew in freezer containers. To use, partially thaw in refrigerator overnight. Heat in a saucepan, stirring occasionally; add a little water if necessary.*

GREAT NORTHERN BEAN STEW

OTHER MAKE-AHEAD MEALS

Breakfast, brunch, meatless or seafood—browse through these great recipes and find a dish that makes your mouth water. It's just what you're looking for!

FRUIT & NUT BAKED OATMEAL, P. 93

HAM & GRUYERE MINI QUICHES

Because I make this recipe in muffin cups, each person gets their own quiche. I have also doubled the recipe and used jumbo muffin cups—then I bake them about 10 minutes longer.
—**GENA STOUT** RAVENDEN, AR

PREP: 30 MIN. • **BAKE:** 20 MIN.
MAKES: 10 MINI QUICHES

- 4 large eggs, lightly beaten
- 1 cup 2% cottage cheese
- ¼ cup 2% milk
- 2 tablespoons all-purpose flour
- ½ teaspoon baking powder
- ¼ teaspoon ground nutmeg
- ¼ teaspoon pepper
- 1½ cups shredded Gruyere or Swiss cheese
- ¾ cup finely chopped fully cooked ham
- 3 tablespoons thinly sliced green onions

1. Preheat oven to 375°. In a large bowl, combine the first seven ingredients; fold in Gruyere cheese, ham and onions. Fill greased muffin cups three-fourths full.
2. Bake 18-22 minutes or until a knife inserted near the center comes out clean. Cool 5 minutes before removing from pans to wire racks.
FREEZE OPTION *Transfer baked and cooled quiches to a large resealable plastic freezer bag and freeze up to 3 months. To use, thaw in the refrigerator overnight. Preheat oven to 350°. Transfer quiches to a greased baking sheet; bake 10-14 minutes or until heated through.*

HAM & GRUYERE MINI QUICHES

FORGOTTEN JAMBALAYA

caption: FORGOTTEN JAMBALAYA

SLOW COOKER

FORGOTTEN JAMBALAYA

During chilly months, I fix this jambalaya at least once a month. It's so easy...just chop the vegetables, dump everything in the slow cooker and forget it! Even my sons, who are picky about spicy things, love this dish.
—**CINDI COSS** COPPELL, TX

PREP: 35 MIN. • **COOK:** 4¼ HOURS
MAKES: 11 SERVINGS

- 1 can (14½ ounces) diced tomatoes, undrained
- 1 can (14½ ounces) beef or chicken broth
- 1 can (6 ounces) tomato paste
- 3 celery ribs, chopped
- 2 medium green peppers, chopped
- 1 medium onion, chopped
- 5 garlic cloves, minced
- 3 teaspoons dried parsley flakes
- 2 teaspoons dried basil
- 1½ teaspoons dried oregano
- 1¼ teaspoons salt
- ½ teaspoon cayenne pepper
- ½ teaspoon hot pepper sauce
- 1 pound boneless skinless chicken breasts, cut into 1-inch cubes
- 1 pound smoked sausage, halved and cut into ¼-inch slices
- ½ pound uncooked medium shrimp, peeled and deveined
  Hot cooked rice

1. In a 5-qt. slow cooker, combine tomatoes, broth and tomato paste. Stir in celery, green peppers, onion, garlic and seasonings. Stir in chicken and sausage.
2. Cover and cook on low for 4-6 hours or until the chicken is no longer pink. Stir in shrimp. Cover and cook 15-30 minutes longer or until shrimp turn pink. Serve with rice.
FREEZE OPTION *Place individual portions of cooled stew in freezer containers and freeze. To use, partially thaw in refrigerator overnight. Heat through in a saucepan, stirring occasionally and adding a little water if necessary.*

BAKED BLUEBERRY-MASCARPONE FRENCH TOAST

When I want something special to serve for a weekend brunch, I turn to this never-fail recipe. It's wonderful during the spring and early summer, when the blueberries are particularly good.

—PATRICIA QUINN OMAHA, NE

PREP: 15 MIN. + CHILLING
BAKE: 1 HOUR + STANDING
MAKES: 10 SERVINGS

- 8 **slices French bread (½ inch thick), cubed (about 4 cups)**
- 2 **cups fresh or frozen blueberries**
- 2 **cartons (8 ounces each) mascarpone cheese**
- ½ **cup confectioners' sugar**
- 10 **slices French bread (1 inch thick)**
- 8 **large eggs**
- 2 **cups half-and-half cream**
- 1 **cup whole milk**
- ⅓ **cup granulated sugar**
- 1 **teaspoon vanilla extract**
  Additional confectioners' sugar
- 1 **cup sliced almonds, toasted**
  Additional fresh blueberries, optional

1. In a greased 13x9-in. baking dish, layer bread cubes and blueberries. In a small bowl, beat mascarpone cheese and confectioners' sugar until smooth; drop by tablespoonfuls over the blueberries. Top with bread slices. In a large bowl, whisk eggs, cream, milk, granulated sugar and vanilla; pour over bread. Refrigerate mixture, covered, overnight.

2. Preheat oven to 350°. Remove French toast from refrigerator while oven heats. Bake, covered, 30 minutes. Bake, uncovered, for 30-40 minutes longer or until puffed and golden and a knife inserted in the center comes out clean.

3. Let stand 10 minutes before serving. Dust with additional confectioners' sugar; sprinkle with almonds. If desired, serve with additional blueberries.

NOTE *To toast nuts, bake in a shallow pan in a 350° oven for 5-10 minutes, or cook in a skillet over low heat until lightly browned, stirring occasionally.*

CAJUN-STYLE BRUNCH BAKE

CAJUN-STYLE BRUNCH BAKE

It's so handy to fix this hearty breakfast casserole the night before and refrigerate it until morning. The recipe was given to me by a co-worker, and it has become a staple in our family!

—KATHIE DEUSSER CHURCH POINT, LA

PREP: 10 MIN. + CHILLING
BAKE: 45 MIN. + STANDING
MAKES: 6 SERVINGS

- 6 **large eggs, lightly beaten**
- 2 **cups 2% milk**
- 1 **pound sliced bacon, cooked and crumbled**
- 6 **slices bread, cubed**
- 1 **medium potato, peeled and diced**
- 1 **cup shredded cheddar cheese**
- ½ **cup finely chopped onion**
- 1 **to 1½ teaspoons Cajun seasoning**
- 1 **teaspoon salt**

1. In a large bowl, combine all the ingredients. Transfer to a greased 11x7-in. baking dish. Cover and refrigerate overnight.

2. Remove from the refrigerator 30 minutes before baking. Bake, uncovered, at 350° for 45-50 minutes or until a knife inserted in the center comes out clean. Let stand for 10 minutes before cutting.

FREEZE OPTION *Cover and freeze unbaked casserole. To use, partially thaw in refrigerator overnight. Remove from refrigerator 30 minutes before baking. Preheat oven to 350°. Bake casserole as directed, increasing time as necessary for a knife inserted in the center to come out clean.*

BAKED BLUEBERRY-MASCARPONE FRENCH TOAST

CLASSIC CRAB CAKES

CLASSIC CRAB CAKES

This region is known for good seafood, and crab cakes are a traditional favorite. I learned to make them from a chef in a restaurant where they were a best seller. The crabmeat's sweet and mild flavor is sparked by the blend of other ingredients.
—DEBBIE TERENZINI LUSBY, MD

START TO FINISH: 20 MIN.
MAKES: 8 SERVINGS

- 1 pound fresh or canned crabmeat, drained, flaked and cartilage removed
- 2 to 2½ cups soft bread crumbs
- 1 large egg, beaten
- ¾ cup mayonnaise
- ⅓ cup each chopped celery, green pepper and onion
- 1 tablespoon seafood seasoning
- 1 tablespoon minced fresh parsley
- 2 teaspoons lemon juice
- 1 teaspoon Worcestershire sauce
- 1 teaspoon prepared mustard
- ¼ teaspoon pepper
- ⅛ teaspoon hot pepper sauce
- 2 to 4 tablespoons vegetable oil, optional
  Lemon wedges, optional

In a large bowl, combine crab, bread crumbs, egg, mayonnaise, vegetables and seasonings. Shape into eight patties. Broil the patties or cook in a skillet in oil for 4 minutes on each side or until golden brown. If desired, serve with lemon.

FREEZE OPTION *Freeze cooled crab cakes in freezer containers, separating layers with waxed paper. To use, reheat on a baking sheet in a preheated 325° oven until heated through.*

BACON-BROCCOLI QUICHE CUPS

Chock-full of veggies and melted cheese, this comforting and colorful egg bake has become a holiday brunch classic.
—IRENE STEINMEYER DENVER, CO

PREP: 10 MIN. • **BAKE:** 25 MIN.
MAKES: 2 SERVINGS

- 4 bacon strips, chopped
- ¼ cup small fresh broccoli florets
- ¼ cup chopped onion
- 1 garlic clove, minced
- 3 large eggs
- 1 tablespoon dried parsley flakes
- ⅛ teaspoon seasoned salt
  Dash pepper
- ¼ cup shredded cheddar cheese
- 2 tablespoons chopped tomato

1. Preheat oven to 400°. In a skillet, cook bacon over medium heat until crisp, stirring occasionally. Remove bacon with a slotted spoon; drain on paper towels. Pour off drippings, reserving 2 teaspoons in pan.
2. Add broccoli and onion to the drippings in the pan; cook and stir for 2-3 minutes or until tender. Add garlic; cook 1 minute longer.
3. In a small bowl, whisk the eggs, parsley, seasoned salt and pepper until blended. Stir in cheese, tomato, bacon and broccoli mixture.
4. Divide the mixture evenly between two 10-oz. ramekins or custard cups coated with cooking spray. Bake 22-25 minutes or until a knife inserted in the center comes out clean.
NOTE *For a tasty variation, try substituting asparagus for broccoli and Swiss for the cheddar cheese.*
FREEZE OPTION *Securely cover and freeze unbaked quiche cups. To use, remove from freezer 30 minutes before baking (do not thaw). Preheat oven to 400°. Bake as directed, increasing time as necessary for a knife inserted near the center to come out clean. Cover loosely with foil if tops brown too quickly.*

✳

TEST KITCHEN TIP To check the freshness of an egg place it in a glass of cold water. A fresh egg will remain on the bottom of the glass. If the egg floats to the surface, it is not fresh and should not be used.

BACON-BROCCOLI QUICHE CUPS

BACON, PEPPERS & EGG BAKE

Whip up this tasty breakfast casserole the night before to make your morning meal a snap. We used peppers, bacon and cheese to lend homestyle appeal.

—*TASTE OF HOME* TEST KITCHEN

PREP: 20 MIN. + CHILLING • **BAKE:** 50 MIN.
MAKES: 12 SERVINGS

- 1 **pound bacon strips, diced**
- ½ **cup julienned sweet orange pepper**
- ½ **cup julienned sweet red pepper**
- 6 **cups cubed day-old bread**
- 1½ **cups shredded Mexican cheese blend**
- 9 **large eggs, lightly beaten**
- 2 **cups milk**
- 1 **can (4 ounces) chopped green chilies**
- 1½ **teaspoons chili powder**
- 1 **teaspoon ground cumin**
  Salsa and sour cream, optional

1. In a large skillet, cook bacon over medium heat until crisp. Using a slotted spoon, remove bacon to paper towels. Pour off drippings, reserving 1 tablespoon in the pan. Saute sweet peppers in drippings until tender; transfer to a large bowl. Stir in bacon, bread and cheese.

2. In another large bowl, combine eggs, milk, chilies, chili powder and cumin. Pour over the bread mixture; gently stir to combine. Transfer to a greased 13x9-in. baking dish. Cover and refrigerate overnight.

3. Remove from the refrigerator 30 minutes before baking. Preheat oven to 350°. Bake, uncovered, 50-55 minutes or until a knife inserted in the center comes out clean. Let stand 5 minutes before serving. If desired, serve with salsa and sour cream.

FREEZE OPTION *Cover and freeze unbaked casserole for up to 3 months. To use, completely thaw in the refrigerator overnight. Remove from the refrigerator 30 minutes before baking. Preheat oven to 350°. Bake, uncovered, 50-60 minutes or until a knife inserted in the center comes out clean. Let stand for 5 minutes before serving. Serve as directed.*

BACON, PEPPERS & EGG BAKE

THREE-CHEESE SOUFFLES

No matter when I've made these souffles, they have always been a success. I've never seen the centers start to fall, but it's best to plan on serving them hot from the oven.

—JEAN FERENCE SHERWOOD PARK, AB

PREP: 40 MIN. + COOLING • **BAKE:** 40 MIN.
MAKES: 8 SERVINGS

- ⅓ cup butter, cubed
- ⅓ cup all-purpose flour
- 2 cups whole milk
- 1 teaspoon Dijon mustard
- ¼ teaspoon salt
  Dash hot pepper sauce
- 1½ cups shredded Swiss cheese
- 1 cup shredded cheddar cheese
- ¼ cup shredded Parmesan cheese
- 6 large eggs
- ½ teaspoon cream of tartar

1. In a small saucepan, melt butter over medium heat. Stir in flour until smooth; cook 1 minute. Gradually whisk in the milk, mustard, salt and pepper sauce. Bring to a boil, stirring constantly; cook and stir 1-2 minutes or until thickened. Reduce heat to medium-low; stir in cheeses until melted. Transfer to a large bowl.
2. Separate eggs. Place egg whites in a medium bowl; let stand at room temperature 30 minutes. Meanwhile, in a small bowl, beat egg yolks until thick and lemon-colored, about 4 minutes. Stir in ⅓ cup hot cheese mixture; return all to remaining cheese mixture, stirring constantly. Cool completely, about 30 minutes.
3. Preheat oven to 325°. Place eight ungreased 8-oz. ramekins in a baking pan.
4. With clean beaters, beat egg whites with cream of tartar on high speed until stiff but not dry. With a rubber spatula, gently stir a fourth of the egg whites into the cheese mixture. Fold in the remaining whites.
5. Transfer to prepared ramekins. Add 1 in. of hot water to the baking pan. Bake 40-45 minutes or until tops are golden brown. Serve immediately.
FREEZE OPTION *Securely wrap unbaked souffles with foil and freeze. To use, preheat oven to 325°. Remove foil and place frozen souffles in a baking pan; add 1 in. warm water to the baking pan. Bake 60-65 minutes or until heated through and tops are golden brown.*

(5) INGREDIENTS
TOMATO & GARLIC BUTTER BEAN DINNER

For those days when I get home late and just want a warm meal, I stir up tomatoes, garlic and butter beans. Ladle it over some noodles if you're in the mood for pasta—it makes a great sauce!

—JESSICA MEYERS AUSTIN, TX

START TO FINISH: 15 MIN.
MAKES: 4 SERVINGS

- 1 tablespoon olive oil
- 2 garlic cloves, minced
- 2 cans (14½ ounces) no-salt-added petite diced tomatoes, undrained
- 1 can (16 ounces) butter beans, rinsed and drained
- 6 cups fresh baby spinach (about 6 ounces)
- ½ teaspoon Italian seasoning
- ¼ teaspoon pepper
  Hot cooked pasta and grated Parmesan cheese, optional

In a large skillet, heat the oil over medium-high heat. Add garlic; cook and stir 30-45 seconds or until tender. Add tomatoes, beans, spinach, Italian seasoning and pepper; cook until spinach is wilted, stirring occasionally. If desired, serve with pasta and cheese.
FREEZE OPTION *Freeze cooled bean mixture in freezer containers. To use, partially thaw in refrigerator overnight. Heat through in a saucepan, stirring occasionally and adding a little water if necessary.*

THREE-CHEESE SOUFFLES

OVERNIGHT SPINACH MANICOTTI

A friend gave me an awesome recipe for manicotti...and I set out to make it a little healthier. Now, whenever we have company, my husband asks me to serve this. Even our 2-year-old son loves it!
—TONYA FITZGERALD WEST MONROE, LA

PREP: 10 MIN. + CHILLING • **BAKE:** 40 MIN.
MAKES: 7 SERVINGS

- 1 carton (15 ounces) reduced-fat ricotta cheese
- 1 package (10 ounces) frozen chopped spinach, thawed and squeezed dry
- 1½ cups shredded part-skim mozzarella cheese, divided
- ½ cup grated Parmesan cheese, divided
- 2 large egg whites
- 2 teaspoons minced fresh parsley
- ½ teaspoon salt
- ½ teaspoon onion powder
- ½ teaspoon pepper
- ¼ teaspoon garlic powder
- 4½ cups meatless spaghetti sauce
- ¾ cup water
- 1 package (8 ounces) manicotti shells

1. In a large bowl, combine ricotta cheese, spinach, 1 cup mozzarella cheese, ¼ cup Parmesan cheese, egg whites, parsley, salt, onion powder, pepper and garlic powder. Combine spaghetti sauce and water; spread 1 cup in an ungreased 13x9-in. baking dish. Stuff uncooked manicotti shells with the ricotta mixture; arrange over the tomato sauce. Top with remaining sauce. Cover manicotti and refrigerate overnight.
2. Remove from the refrigerator 30 minutes before baking. Sprinkle with the remaining mozzarella and Parmesan cheeses. Bake, uncovered, at 350° for 40-45 minutes or until heated through.

SHRIMP & BROCCOLI BROWN RICE PAELLA

FREEZE IT

Place cooled paella in freezer containers. To use, partially thaw in refrigerator overnight. Microwave, covered, on high in a microwave-safe dish until heated through, stirring gently and adding a little stock or water if necessary.

SHRIMP & BROCCOLI BROWN RICE PAELLA

Years ago, when my husband and I were vacationing in France, we came across an open market where a fellow from Spain was making paella in a skillet; we've been hooked ever since. I love to whip this up for a large group, but if the gathering is small, I know I can easily freeze leftovers for another time.
—JONI HILTON ROCKLIN, CA

PREP: 45 MIN. • **COOK:** 50 MIN.
MAKES: 8 SERVINGS

- 1 tablespoon olive oil
- 1 medium onion, chopped
- 1 medium sweet red pepper, chopped
- 1 cup sliced fresh mushrooms
- 2 cups uncooked long grain brown rice
- 2 garlic cloves, minced
- 2 teaspoons paprika
- ½ teaspoon salt
- ½ teaspoon cayenne pepper
- ¼ teaspoon saffron threads
- 6 cups chicken stock
- 2 pounds uncooked large shrimp, peeled and deveined
- 1½ cups fresh broccoli florets
- 1 cup frozen peas

1. In a Dutch oven, heat oil over medium-high heat. Add onion, red pepper and mushrooms; cook and stir 6-8 minutes or until tender. Stir in rice, garlic and seasonings; cook 1-2 minutes longer.
2. Stir in stock; bring to a boil. Reduce heat; simmer, covered, 40-45 minutes or until liquid is absorbed and rice is tender. Add shrimp and broccoli; cook 8-10 minutes longer or until shrimp turn pink. Stir in peas; heat through.

EGG & SPINACH BREAKFAST BURRITOS

EGG & SPINACH BREAKFAST BURRITOS

When we camp out, we want our meals ready in a hurry. We make these hearty burritos at home, freeze them and reheat over the campfire.

—**KRISTEN STECKLEIN** WAUKESHA, WI

START TO FINISH: 30 MIN.
MAKES: 10 SERVINGS

- 1 pound bulk lean turkey breakfast sausage
- 1 tablespoon canola oil
- 1 cup frozen cubed hash brown potatoes, thawed
- 1 small red onion, chopped
- 1 small sweet red pepper, chopped
- 6 cups (about 4 ounces) fresh spinach, coarsely chopped
- 6 large eggs, beaten
- 10 multigrain tortillas (8 inches), warmed
- ¾ cup crumbled queso fresco or feta cheese
   Guacamole and salsa, optional

1. In a nonstick skillet, cook sausage over medium heat until no longer pink, 4-6 minutes, breaking into crumbles; remove from pan.
2. In the same skillet, heat oil. Add potatoes, onion and pepper; cook, stirring, until tender, 5-7 minutes. Add spinach; stir until wilted, 1-2 minutes. Add sausage and eggs; cook and stir until no liquid egg remains.
3. Spoon ½ cup filling across center of each tortilla; sprinkle with cheese. Fold bottom and sides over filling and roll up. If desired, serve burritos with guacamole and salsa.

FREEZE OPTION *Cool filling before making burritos. Individually wrap burritos in foil and freeze in a resealable plastic freezer bag for up to 1 month. To use, partially thaw overnight in refrigerator or cooler. Prepare campfire or grill for medium heat. Place foil-wrapped burritos on a grill grate over a campfire or on grill. Grill until heated through, 25-30 minutes, turning occasionally.*

BREAKFAST SAUSAGE BREAD

Any time we take this savory, satisfying bread to a potluck, we never bring any home! My husband usually makes it; he prides himself on the beautiful golden loaves. If we're making it for ourselves, we'll freeze the second loaf to save for when we want something special!

—**SHIRLEY CALDWELL** NORTHWOOD, OH

PREP: 25 MIN. + RISING • **BAKE:** 25 MIN.
MAKES: 2 LOAVES (16 SLICES EACH)

- 2 loaves (1 pound each) frozen white bread dough, thawed
- ½ pound mild pork sausage
- ½ pound bulk spicy pork sausage
- 1½ cups diced fresh mushrooms
- ½ cup chopped onion
- 3 large eggs, divided use
- 2½ cups (10 ounces) shredded mozzarella cheese
- 1 teaspoon dried basil
- 1 teaspoon dried parsley flakes
- 1 teaspoon dried rosemary, crushed
- 1 teaspoon garlic powder

1. Cover dough and let rise in a warm place until doubled. Preheat oven to 350°. In a large skillet, cook sausage, mushrooms and onion over medium-high heat for 6-8 minutes or until the sausage is no longer pink, breaking up the sausage into crumbles. Drain. Transfer to a bowl; cool.
2. Stir in two eggs, cheese and seasonings. Roll each loaf of dough into a 16x12-in. rectangle. Spread half of the sausage mixture over each rectangle to within 1 in. of edges. Roll up jelly-roll style, starting with a short side; pinch seams to seal. Place on a greased baking sheet.
3. In a small bowl, whisk remaining egg. Brush over tops. Bake 25-30 minutes or until golden brown. Serve warm.

FREEZE OPTION *Securely wrap and freeze cooled loaves in foil and place in resealable plastic freezer bags. To use, place foil-wrapped loaf on a baking sheet and reheat in a 450° oven 10-15 minutes or until heated through. Carefully remove foil; return to oven a few minutes longer until crust is crisp.*

BREAKFAST SAUSAGE BREAD

FOUR-CHEESE
STUFFED SHELLS

SLOW COOKER
RED CLAM SAUCE

This luscious sauce tastes like you've worked on it all day. Instead, it cooks hands-free while you do other things. What a great way to jazz up pasta!

—JOANN BROWN LATROBE, PA

PREP: 25 MIN. • **COOK:** 3 HOURS
MAKES: 4 SERVINGS

- 1 medium onion, chopped
- 1 tablespoon canola oil
- 2 garlic cloves, minced
- 2 cans (6½ ounces each) chopped clams, undrained
- 1 can (14½ ounces) diced tomatoes, undrained
- 1 can (6 ounces) tomato paste
- ¼ cup minced fresh parsley
- 1 bay leaf
- 1 teaspoon sugar
- 1 teaspoon dried basil
- ½ teaspoon dried thyme
- 6 ounces linguine, cooked and drained

1. In a small skillet, saute the onion in oil until tender. Add garlic; cook 1 minute longer.

2. Transfer to a 1½- or 2-qt. slow cooker. Stir in the clams, tomatoes, tomato paste, parsley, bay leaf, sugar, basil and thyme.

3. Cover and cook on low for 3-4 hours or until heated through. Discard bay leaf. Serve with linguine.

FREEZE OPTION *Cool before placing in a freezer container. Cover and freeze for up to 3 months. To use, thaw in the refrigerator overnight. Place in a large saucepan; heat through, stirring occasionally. Serve with linguine.*

RED CLAM SAUCE

FOUR-CHEESE STUFFED SHELLS

Because one or two kinds of cheese just isn't enough, we came up with these satisfying shells, bursting with ricotta, Asiago, mozzarella and cottage cheese. Use your favorite brand of spaghetti sauce, meatless or not.

—TASTE OF HOME TEST KITCHEN

PREP: 20 MIN. • **BAKE:** 25 MIN.
MAKES: 2 SERVINGS

- 6 uncooked jumbo pasta shells
- ½ cup shredded part-skim mozzarella cheese, divided
- ¼ cup shredded Asiago cheese
- ¼ cup ricotta cheese
- ¼ cup 4% cottage cheese
- 1 tablespoon minced chives
- 1 package (10 ounces) frozen chopped spinach, thawed and squeezed dry
- 1 cup meatless spaghetti sauce

1. Cook pasta according to package directions. Meanwhile, in a small bowl, combine ¼ cup mozzarella cheese, Asiago cheese, ricotta cheese, cottage cheese, chives and ½ cup spinach (save the remaining spinach for another use).

2. Spread ½ cup spaghetti sauce into a shallow 1½-qt. baking dish coated with cooking spray. Drain pasta; stuff with cheese mixture. Arrange in prepared dish. Top with remaining spaghetti sauce and mozzarella.

3. Cover and bake at 350° for 25-30 minutes or until heated through.

FREEZE OPTION *Cool stuffed, unbaked pasta shells; cover and freeze. To use, partially thaw in refrigerator overnight. Remove from refrigerator 30 minutes before baking. Preheat oven to 350°. Bake as directed, increasing time as necessary to heat through and for a thermometer inserted in the center to read 165° (test 2 or 3 shells).*

OVEN-FRIED FISH NUGGETS

My husband and I love fried fish, but we're both trying to cut back on dietary fat. I made up this recipe, and it's a hit with us both. He says he likes it as much as deep-fried fish, and that's saying a lot!

—LADONNA REED PONCA CITY, OK

START TO FINISH: 25 MIN.
MAKES: 4 SERVINGS

- ⅓ cup seasoned bread crumbs
- ⅓ cup crushed cornflakes
- 3 tablespoons grated Parmesan cheese
- ½ teaspoon salt
- ¼ teaspoon pepper
- 1½ pounds cod fillets, cut into 1-inch cubes
  Butter-flavored cooking spray

1. In a shallow bowl, combine bread crumbs, cornflakes, Parmesan cheese, salt and pepper. Coat the fish with butter-flavored spray, then roll in crumb mixture.
2. Place on a baking sheet coated with cooking spray. Bake at 375° for 15-20 minutes or until fish flakes easily with a fork.

OVEN-FRIED CHICKEN NUGGETS
Substitute cubed boneless skinless chicken breasts for the cod. Bake as directed until chicken is no longer pink.

FRUIT & NUT BAKED OATMEAL

FRUIT & NUT BAKED OATMEAL

In this part of the Midwest, baked oatmeal is a Mennonite speciality. My daughters are always delighted if we have leftovers for them to take home.

—FANCHEON RESLER ALBION, IN

PREP: 15 MIN. • **BAKE:** 35 MIN.
MAKES: 8 SERVINGS

- 6 cups quick-cooking oats
- 4 teaspoons baking powder
- 1 teaspoon ground cinnamon
- 4 large eggs
- 2 cups 2% milk
- 1½ cups packed brown sugar
- 1 cup canola oil
- 1 cup shredded apple
- 1 cup dried cranberries
- ½ cup chopped walnuts, toasted
  Additional 2% milk

1. Preheat oven to 400°. Mix oats, baking powder and cinnamon. In another bowl, whisk eggs, milk, brown sugar and oil until blended; stir into oat mixture. Fold in apple, cranberries and walnuts.
2. Transfer to a greased 13x9-in. baking dish. Bake, uncovered, until set and edges are lightly browned, 35-40 minutes. Slice; serve with milk.
FREEZE OPTION *Freeze cooled individual pieces on waxed paper-lined baking sheets until firm. Transfer to resealable plastic freezer bags; return to freezer. To use, microwave each piece on high until heated through, 1-2 minutes.*

FREEZE IT

Cover and freeze unbaked fish nuggets on a waxed paper-lined baking sheet until firm. Transfer to a resealable plastic freezer bag; return to freezer. To use, preheat oven to 375°. Bake nuggets on a rack on a greased baking sheet 15-20 minutes or until fish flakes easily with a fork.

OVEN-FRIED FISH NUGGETS

pineapple, ¼ cup flaked coconut and ¼ cup chopped macadamia nuts.

BLUEBERRY WAFFLES *Increase baking powder to 2½ teaspoons. Before adding egg whites, fold in 1½ cups fresh or frozen blueberries.*

CINNAMON WAFFLES *Substitute brown sugar for sugar. With flour, stir in ½ teaspoon of ground cinnamon. With egg yolk, stir in ¾ teaspoon of vanilla.*

SCRAMBLED EGG MUFFINS

After enjoying scrambled egg muffins at a local restaurant, I came up with this savory version that my husband likes even better. Freeze the extras to reheat on busy mornings.

—**CATHY LARKINS** MARSHFIELD, MO

START TO FINISH: 30 MIN.
MAKES: 1 DOZEN

- ½ **pound bulk pork sausage**
- 12 **large eggs**
- ½ **cup chopped onion**
- ¼ **cup chopped green pepper**
- ½ **teaspoon salt**
- ¼ **teaspoon garlic powder**
- ¼ **teaspoon pepper**
- ½ **cup shredded cheddar cheese**

1. Preheat oven to 350°. In a large skillet, cook sausage over medium heat until no longer pink; drain.
2. In a large bowl, beat eggs. Add onion, green pepper, salt, garlic powder and pepper. Stir in the sausage and cheese.
3. Spoon by ⅓ cupfuls into muffin cups coated with cooking spray. Bake for 20-25 minutes or until a knife inserted near the center comes out clean.

FREEZE IT

Cool baked egg muffins. Cover and place on waxed paper-lined baking sheets and freeze until firm. Transfer to resealable plastic freezer bags; return to freezer. To use, place in greased muffin pan, cover loosely with foil and reheat in a preheated 350° oven until heated through. Or microwave each muffin on high 30-60 seconds or until heated through.

FLUFFY WAFFLES

A friend shared the recipe for these light and delicious waffles. The cinnamon cream syrup is a nice change from maple syrup, and it keeps quite well in the fridge. Our two children also like it on toast.

—**AMY GILLES** ELLSWORTH, WI

PREP: 25 MIN. • **COOK:** 20 MIN.
MAKES: 10 WAFFLES (6½ INCHES)
AND 1⅔ CUPS SYRUP

- 2 **cups all-purpose flour**
- 1 **tablespoon sugar**
- 2 **teaspoons baking powder**
- ½ **teaspoon salt**
- 3 **large eggs, separated**
- 2 **cups milk**
- ¼ **cup canola oil**

CINNAMON CREAM SYRUP

- 1 **cup sugar**
- ½ **cup light corn syrup**
- ¼ **cup water**
- 1 **can (5 ounces) evaporated milk**
- 1 **teaspoon vanilla extract**
- ½ **teaspoon ground cinnamon**

1. In a bowl, combine flour, sugar, baking powder and salt. Combine egg yolks, milk and oil; stir into the dry ingredients just until moistened. In a small bowl, beat egg whites until stiff peaks form; fold into batter. Bake in a preheated waffle iron according to manufacturer's directions.
2. Meanwhile, for syrup, combine sugar, corn syrup and water in a saucepan. Bring to a boil over medium heat; cook and stir for 2 minutes or until thickened. Remove from the heat; stir in the milk, vanilla and cinnamon. Serve with waffles.

FREEZE OPTION *Cool waffles on wire racks. Freeze between layers of waxed paper in a resealable plastic freezer bag. Reheat waffles in a toaster on medium setting. Or microwave each waffle on high for 30-60 seconds or until heated through.*

HAM & CHEESE WAFFLES *Omit sugar and Cinnamon Cream Syrup. Increase flour to 2½ cups. Fold in 1½ cups shredded mozzarella cheese and ½ cup cubed fully cooked ham.*

TROPICAL WAFFLES *Omit Cinnamon Cream Syrup. Increase baking powder to 4 teaspoons. Before adding egg whites, stir in 1 can (8 oz.) well-drained crushed*

SPINACH CHEESE PHYLLO SQUARES

A higher-fat version of this casserole was a big hit when my aunt and I ran a gourmet carryout business. This is my lightened-up treatment to serve at home!

—**JULIE REMER** GAHANNA, OH

PREP: 20 MIN. + CHILLING
BAKE: 40 MIN. + STANDING
MAKES: 12 SERVINGS

- 6 sheets phyllo dough (14 inches x 9 inches)
- 1 package (10 ounces) frozen chopped spinach, thawed and squeezed dry
- 2½ cups shredded part-skim mozzarella cheese
- 1½ cups shredded reduced-fat cheddar cheese
- 1½ cups fat-free cottage cheese
- 4 large eggs
- 1½ teaspoons dried parsley flakes
- ¾ teaspoon salt
- 6 large egg whites
- 1½ cups fat-free milk

1. Layer three phyllo sheets in a 13x9-in. baking dish coated with cooking spray, lightly spraying the top of each sheet with cooking spray.
2. In a large bowl, combine spinach, cheese, 2 eggs, parsley flakes and salt; spread over the phyllo dough. Top with the remaining phyllo sheets, lightly spraying the top of each sheet with cooking spray. Using a sharp knife, cut into 12 squares; cover and chill for 1 hour.
3. In a large bowl, beat egg whites, milk and the remaining eggs until blended; pour over casserole. Cover and refrigerate overnight.
4. Remove from the refrigerator 1 hour before baking. Bake casserole, uncovered, at 375° for 40-50 minutes or until a knife inserted near the center comes out clean. Let stand for 10 minutes before cutting.

DE-LIGHTFUL TUNA CASSEROLE

This lightened-up tuna casserole will satisfy your family's craving for comfort food with fewer unwanted calories and less fat!

—**COLLEEN WILLEY** HAMBURG, NY

PREP: 15 MIN. • **BAKE:** 25 MIN.
MAKES: 5 SERVINGS

- 1 package (7 ounces) elbow macaroni
- 1 can (10¾ ounces) reduced-fat reduced-sodium condensed cream of mushroom soup, undiluted
- 1 cup sliced fresh mushrooms
- 1 cup shredded reduced-fat cheddar cheese
- 1 cup fat-free milk
- 1 can (5 ounces) light water-packed tuna, drained and flaked
- 2 tablespoons diced pimientos
- 3 teaspoons dried minced onion
- 1 teaspoon ground mustard
- ¼ teaspoon salt
- ⅓ cup crushed cornflakes

1. Cook macaroni according to package directions. Meanwhile, in a large bowl, combine soup, mushrooms, cheese, milk, tuna, pimientos, onion, mustard and salt. Drain the macaroni; add to the tuna mixture and mix well.
2. Transfer to a 2-qt. baking dish coated with cooking spray. Sprinkle with cornflakes. Bake the casserole, uncovered, at 350° for 25-30 minutes or until bubbly.

FREEZE OPTION *Cool unbaked casserole before topping with cornflakes; cover and freeze. To use, partially thaw in refrigerator overnight. Remove from refrigerator 30 minutes before baking. Preheat oven to 350°. Top casserole with cornflakes and bake as directed; increase time as necessary to heat through and for a thermometer inserted in center to read 165°.*

DE-LIGHTFUL TUNA CASSEROLE

SWEET TREATS

Whether it's a stunning cheesecake you made the night before, a tangy sherbet that's waiting in the freezer or cookie dough you can bake at a moment's notice, you'll always have time to indulge your sweet tooth!

PEANUT BUTTER CREAM PIE, P. 103

LEMON POUND CAKE LOAVES

LEMON POUND CAKE LOAVES

Next time you are spending the weekend at a friend's house, take these luscious lemon loaves with you. You can have them for breakfast the next morning!
—**LOLA BAXTER** WINNEBAGO, MN

PREP: 20 MIN. • **BAKE:** 35 MIN. + COOLING
MAKES: 2 MINI LOAVES (6 SLICES EACH)

- ½ cup butter, softened
- 1 cup sugar
- 2 large eggs
- 1 teaspoon grated lemon peel
- 1 teaspoon vanilla extract
- ½ teaspoon lemon extract
- 1¾ cups all-purpose flour
- ½ teaspoon salt
- ¼ teaspoon baking soda
- ½ cup sour cream

ICING
- ¾ cup confectioners' sugar
- ½ teaspoon grated lemon peel
- 1 tablespoon lemon juice

1. Preheat oven to 350°. Grease and flour two 5¾x3x2-in. loaf pans.
2. In a large bowl, cream butter and sugar until light and fluffy. Add eggs, one at a time, beating well after each addition. Beat in lemon peel and extracts. In another bowl, whisk flour, salt and baking soda; add to creamed mixture alternately with sour cream, beating well after each addition.
3. Transfer to prepared pans. Bake 35-40 minutes or until a toothpick inserted in center comes out clean. Cool in pans for 10 minutes before removing the loaves to wire racks to cool completely.
4. In a small bowl, mix the icing ingredients. Spoon over loaves.
FOR ONE LARGE LOAF *Make batter as directed; transfer to a greased and floured 8x4-in. loaf pan. Bake in a preheated 350° oven for 40-45 minutes or until a toothpick comes out clean. Proceed as directed.*

MINT-FILLED COOKIES

I tuck a peppermint patty inside these treats for a surprise. The bites will melt in your mouth.
—**KAREN NIELSON** ST. GEORGE, UT

PREP: 30 MIN. + CHILLING
BAKE: 10 MIN./BATCH + COOLING
MAKES: ABOUT 3 DOZEN

- 1 cup butter, softened
- 4 ounces cream cheese, softened
- 1 cup sugar
- ½ cup packed brown sugar
- 2 large eggs
- 1 tablespoon 2% milk
- 1 teaspoon vanilla extract
- 4 cups all-purpose flour
- 1 teaspoon baking soda
- ½ teaspoon salt
- 40 chocolate-covered peppermint patties (1½ inches), unwrapped
- ¾ cup semisweet chocolate chips
- 1 tablespoon shortening

1. In a large bowl, cream butter, cream cheese and sugars until light and fluffy. Beat in eggs, milk and vanilla. In another bowl, whisk flour, baking soda and salt; gradually beat into butter mixture.
2. Divide dough in half. Shape each into a disk; wrap in plastic wrap. Refrigerate 30 minutes or until firm enough to roll.
3. Preheat oven to 400°. On a lightly floured surface, roll each portion of dough to ¼-in. thickness. Cut with a floured 3-in. round cookie cutter. Place a mint patty in center of each circle; fold dough over patty. Pinch to seal seams. Place on greased baking sheets, seam side down.
4. Bake 8-10 minutes or until cookies are golden brown. Remove from pans to wire racks to cool completely.
5. In a microwave, melt chocolate chips and shortening; stir until smooth. Drizzle over cookies. Refrigerate until set. Store in an airtight container in the refrigerator.
FREEZE OPTION *Transfer disks of unbaked dough to a resealable plastic freezer bag; freeze. To use, thaw dough in refrigerator until soft enough to roll. Prepare, bake and decorate as directed.*

MINT-FILLED COOKIES

CAFE MOCHA PINWHEELS

CAFE MOCHA PINWHEELS

When my daughter was young, I made these cookies for school bake sales. Preschoolers enjoy rolling up the dough, and older kids can get in on all the steps.
—**DION FRISCHER** ANN ARBOR, MI

PREP: 30 MIN. + FREEZING
BAKE: 10 MIN./BATCH
MAKES: ABOUT 4½ DOZEN

- 1 cup butter, softened
- 2 cups sugar
- 2 large eggs
- 2 teaspoons vanilla extract
- 3 cups all-purpose flour
- 2 teaspoons baking powder
- 1 tablespoon instant espresso powder
- ½ cup baking cocoa

1. In a large bowl, cream butter and sugar until light and fluffy. Beat in eggs and vanilla. In another bowl, whisk the flour, baking powder and espresso powder; gradually beat into creamed mixture. Divide dough in half. Beat cocoa into half of dough. Divide each color into two portions.
2. On baking sheets, roll each portion between two sheets of waxed paper into a 9x7-in. rectangle. Remove waxed paper. Place one chocolate rectangle on top of one plain rectangle. Roll up tightly jelly-roll style, starting with a long side. Tightly roll waxed paper over dough, using the waxed paper to mold the dough into a smooth roll. Securely wrap waxed paper-covered roll in plastic wrap; repeat with remaining dough. Freeze 1 hour or until firm.
3. Preheat oven to 350°. Unwrap and cut dough crosswise into ¼-in. slices. Place 2 in. apart on ungreased baking sheets. Bake 10-12 minutes or until edges are light brown. Cool on pans 2 minutes. Remove to wire racks to cool.
 FREEZE OPTION *Place wrapped logs in a resealable plastic freezer bag before freezing. To use, unwrap frozen logs and cut into slices. If necessary, let dough stand 15 minutes at room temperature before cutting. Bake as directed.*

APPLE-PEAR COMPOTE

Apples and pears are popular fruits, so this treat is great for brunch buffets. For a tasty addition, I like to add raisins or chopped nuts to the compote. Sometimes I even stir in ⅓ cup brandy or rum!
—**NANCY HEISHMAN** LAS VEGAS, NV

PREP: 20 MIN. • **COOK:** 3¼ HOURS
MAKES: 8 CUPS

- 5 medium apples, peeled and chopped
- 3 medium pears, chopped
- 1 medium orange, thinly sliced
- ½ cup dried cranberries
- ½ cup packed brown sugar
- ½ cup maple syrup
- ⅓ cup butter, cubed
- 2 tablespoons lemon juice
- 2 teaspoons ground cinnamon
- 1 teaspoon ground ginger
- 5 tablespoons orange juice, divided
- 4 teaspoons cornstarch
  Sweetened whipped cream and toasted chopped pecans, optional

1. In a 4- or 5-qt. slow cooker, combine the first 10 ingredients. Stir in 2 tablespoons orange juice. Cook, covered, on low 3-4 hours or until fruit is tender.
2. In a small bowl, mix cornstarch and remaining orange juice until smooth; gradually stir into the fruit mixture. Cook, covered, on high 15-20 minutes longer or until sauce is thickened. If desired, top with whipped cream and pecans.
FREEZE OPTION *Freeze cooled compote in freezer containers. To use, partially thaw in refrigerator overnight. Heat through in a saucepan, stirring occasionally and adding a little orange juice if necessary.*

✱

TEST KITCHEN TIP To avoid getting a small hole in the center of your rolled cookies, cut one edge of the stacked dough at an angle, then roll inward from that edge. The beveled edge will make a tighter fit at the center.

BLUEBERRY QUICK BREAD WITH VANILLA SAUCE

I really love fruit, so I stirred 2 cups of blueberries into a plain quickbread recipe—the result was amazing! The vanilla sauce makes it sweet, almost like dessert. I suggest serving it with morning coffee.

—**SUE DAVIS** WAUSAU, WI

PREP: 20 MIN. • **BAKE:** 50 MIN. + COOLING
MAKES: 8 SERVINGS (2 CUPS SAUCE)

- 1 **large egg**
- 1 **cup milk**
- 3 **tablespoons vegetable oil**
- 2 **cups all-purpose flour**
- 1 **cup sugar**
- 2½ **teaspoons baking powder**
- ½ **teaspoon salt**
- 2 **cups fresh or frozen blueberries**

VANILLA SAUCE

- 1 **cup sugar**
- 1 **tablespoon cornstarch**
- 1 **cup heavy whipping cream**
- ½ **cup butter, cubed**
- 1 **teaspoon vanilla extract**

1. In a large bowl, beat egg, milk and oil. Combine flour, sugar, baking powder and salt; gradually add to the egg mixture, beating just until combined. Fold in blueberries.

2. Pour into a greased 9x5-in. loaf pan. Bake at 350° for 50-55 minutes or until a toothpick inserted near the center comes out clean. Cool for 10 minutes before removing from pan to a wire rack to cool completely.

3. For sauce, combine sugar and cornstarch in a saucepan. Stir in cream until smooth; add butter. Bring to a boil over medium heat; cook and stir for 2 minutes or until thickened. Stir in vanilla. Serve with blueberry bread.

FREEZE OPTION *Securely wrap cooled loaf in plastic wrap and foil; freeze. To use, thaw at room temperature. Prepare sauce as directed and serve with bread.*

NOTE *If using frozen blueberries, use without thawing to avoid discoloring the batter.*

BLUEBERRY QUICK BREAD WITH VANILLA SAUCE

LIME SHORTBREAD
WITH DRIED CHERRIES

LIME SHORTBREAD WITH DRIED CHERRIES

This fresh, sweet-tart cookie also works with dried cranberries and orange zest. I freeze the dough for up to a month.
—**ABIGAIL BOSTWICK** TOMAHAWK, WI

PREP: 25 MIN. + CHILLING
BAKE: 10 MIN./BATCH
MAKES: ABOUT 4½ DOZEN

- 1 **cup butter, softened**
- ¾ **cup confectioners' sugar**
- 1 **tablespoon grated lime peel**
- 2 **teaspoons vanilla extract**
- ½ **teaspoon almond extract**
- 2 **cups all-purpose flour**
- ¼ **teaspoon baking powder**
- ⅛ **teaspoon salt**
- ½ **cup chopped dried cherries**

1. In a large bowl, cream butter and confectioners' sugar until blended. Beat in lime peel and extracts. In another bowl, mix the flour, baking powder and salt; gradually beat into creamed mixture. Stir in cherries.
2. Divide dough in half; shape each into a 7-in.-long roll. Wrap in plastic; refrigerate 3-4 hours or until firm.
3. Preheat oven to 350°. Unwrap and cut dough crosswise into ¼-in. slices.

Place 2 in. apart on ungreased baking sheets. Bake 9-11 minutes or until edges are golden brown. Remove from pans to wire racks to cool.
FREEZE OPTION *Place wrapped logs in resealable plastic freezer bag; freeze. To use, unwrap frozen logs and cut into slices. If necessary, let dough stand a few minutes at room temperature before cutting. Bake as directed.*
ORANGE SHORTBREAD WITH DRIED CRANBERRIES *Substitute grated orange peel for the lime peel and chopped dried cranberries for the cherries.*

NEW ORLEANS BEIGNETS

These sweet French doughnuts are square instead of round and have no hole in the middle. They're a traditional and unmissable part of breakfast in New Orleans.
—**BETH DAWSON** JACKSON, LA

PREP: 25 MIN. + CHILLING
COOK: 5 MIN./BATCH
MAKES: 4 DOZEN

- 1 **package (¼ ounce) active dry yeast**
- ¼ **cup warm water (110° to 115°)**
- 1 **cup evaporated milk**
- ½ **cup canola oil**
- ¼ **cup sugar**
- 1 **large egg**
- 4½ **cups self-rising flour**
   Oil for deep-fat frying
   Confectioners' sugar

1. In a large bowl, dissolve yeast in warm water. Add milk, oil, sugar, egg and 2 cups flour. Beat until smooth. Stir in enough remaining flour to form a soft dough (dough will be sticky). Do not knead. Cover and refrigerate dough overnight.
2. Punch dough down. Turn onto a floured surface; roll into a 16x12-in. rectangle. Cut into 2-in. squares.
3. In an electric skillet or deep-fat fryer, heat oil to 375°. Fry squares, a few at a time, until golden brown on both sides. Drain on paper towels. Roll beignets in confectioners' sugar while still warm.
NOTE *As a substitute for each cup of self-rising flour, place 1½ teaspoons baking powder and ½ teaspoon salt in a measuring cup. Add all-purpose flour to measure 1 cup.*

CHOCOLATE BERRY FREEZE

This lovely make-ahead cake tastes as good as it looks. Rich, creamy and decadent—and ready to be pulled from the freezer at a moment's notice—it's the ideal choice for company.

—LISA RUEHLOW BLAINE, MN

PREP: 20 MIN. + FREEZING
MAKES: 10 SERVINGS

- 2 cups cream-filled chocolate sandwich cookie crumbs
- ½ cup butter, melted
- ¾ cup sweetened condensed milk, divided
- ⅓ cup frozen unsweetened strawberries, thawed and chopped
- 2 tablespoons strawberry ice cream topping
- 1¼ cups heavy whipping cream, whipped, divided
- ⅓ cup slivered almonds, toasted
- 2 tablespoons chocolate syrup

1. Line the bottom and sides of a 9x5-in. loaf pan with heavy-duty foil. Combine cookie crumbs and butter; press half of the mixture into the prepared pan. Freeze for 15 minutes.
2. Pour half of the milk into a small bowl; stir in strawberries and strawberry topping. Fold in half of the whipped cream. Spread over the crust. Sprinkle with the remaining crumb mixture. Freeze for 45-60 minutes or until firm.
3. In a small bowl, combine almonds, chocolate syrup and the remaining milk. Fold in the remaining whipped cream. Spread over the crumb layer (the pan will be full). Cover and freeze for several hours or overnight. May be frozen for up to 2 months.
4. Remove from the freezer 10 minutes before serving. Using foil, lift dessert out of pan. Invert onto a serving platter; discard foil. Cut into slices.

PEANUT BUTTER CREAM PIE

PEANUT BUTTER CREAM PIE

During the warm months, it's nice to have a fluffy, no-bake dessert that's a snap to make. Packed with peanut flavor, this pie gets gobbled up even after a big meal!

—JESSE & ANNE FOUST BLUEFIELD, WV

PREP: 10 MIN. + CHILLING
MAKES: 8 SERVINGS

- 1 package (8 ounces) cream cheese, softened
- ¾ cup confectioners' sugar
- ½ cup peanut butter
- 6 tablespoons milk
- 1 carton (8 ounces) frozen whipped topping, thawed
- 1 graham cracker crust (9 inches)
- ¼ cup chopped peanuts

In a large bowl, beat cream cheese until fluffy. beat in sugar and peanut butter. Gradually add milk. Fold in whipped topping; spoon into the crust. Sprinkle with peanuts. Chill pie overnight.

⑤ INGREDIENTS

CREAMY CITRUS SHERBET

This recipe was handwritten in a booklet that came with my family's first refrigerator in the early 1940s. I was very young at the time, but I can still remember the iceman delivering huge blocks of ice. Since finding the booklet among my mother's things, I make this refreshing dessert often.

—MARIBELLE CULVER GRAND RAPIDS, MI

PREP: 5 MIN. + FREEZING
MAKES: ABOUT 2 QUARTS

- 2 cups sugar
- 1½ cups orange juice
- 5 tablespoons lemon juice
- 4 cups milk

In a large bowl, combine sugar and juices. Gradually add milk. Pour into a 2-qt. freezer container. Freeze for 2 hours, then stir every 30 minutes until slushy. Freeze overnight.

LAYERED LEMON DESSERT SQUARES

I found this recipe in an old cookbook and modified it to be extra citrusy. If you're a fan of key lime pie, change out the lemon flavors for lime.

—DAWN E. LOWENSTEIN
HUNTINGDON VALLEY, PA

PREP: 30 MIN. + CHILLING
MAKES: 12 SERVINGS

- 3½ cups graham cracker crumbs
- 1¾ cups sugar, divided
- 1 tablespoon ground cinnamon
- 1¼ cups butter, melted
- 2 packages (8 ounces each) cream cheese, softened
- 2 cups heavy whipping cream
- 1 teaspoon lemon extract
- 2 jars (10 ounces each) lemon curd or 1 can (15¾ ounces) lemon pie filling

1. In a large bowl, mix cracker crumbs, ¾ cup sugar and cinnamon; stir in butter. Reserve half of mixture for topping. Press remaining crumb mixture onto bottom of a greased 13x9-in. baking dish.

2. In a large bowl, beat cream cheese and remaining sugar until smooth. Gradually beat in cream and extract until soft peaks form. Spread half of the cream cheese mixture over crust. Gently spread lemon curd over cream cheese layer. Spread with remaining cream cheese mixture. Sprinkle with reserved cracker crumbs. Refrigerate, covered, overnight.

FREEZE OPTION *After assembling, cover and freeze the dessert. To use, thaw in the refrigerator overnight.*

RASPBERRY SACHER TORTE

This torte may look like it took hours to make, but it has a surprisingly short list of ingredients. A small slice splendidly satisfies a sweet tooth.

—ROSE HOCKETT COLORADO SPRINGS, CO

PREP: 50 MIN. • **BAKE:** 25 MIN. + STANDING
MAKES: 12 SERVINGS

- 4 large eggs, separated
- 5 tablespoons butter
- ⅔ cup sugar
- 9 ounces bittersweet chocolate, melted
- ¾ cup ground almonds
- ¼ cup all-purpose flour
- ¼ cup seedless raspberry jam

GLAZE

- 3 ounces bittersweet chocolate, chopped
- 2 tablespoons butter

1. Place egg whites in a large bowl; let stand at room temperature for 30 minutes. In a large bowl, beat butter and sugar until crumbly, about 2 minutes. Add egg yolks and melted chocolate; beat on low speed just until combined. Combine almonds and flour; stir into butter mixture just until blended.

2. In another bowl with clean beaters, beat egg whites until stiff peaks form; fold into batter. Transfer to a greased 9-in. springform pan. Bake at 350° for 25-30 minutes or until a toothpick inserted near the center comes out clean. Transfer to a wire rack to cool for 10 minutes. Carefully run a knife around edge of pan to loosen; remove sides of pan. Cool completely.

3. Spread jam over the top of cake. For glaze, in a small saucepan, melt chocolate and butter; spread over the jam. Let stand at room temperature for 1 hour or until set.

FREEZE OPTION *Bake the cake and let cool; do not top with jam. Freeze in a heavy-duty resealable plastic bag for up to 3 months. When ready to use, thaw at room temperature overnight. Top with jam and glaze.*

LAYERED LEMON DESSERT SQUARES

BUTTER PECAN CHEESECAKE

Fall always makes me yearn for this pecan cheesecake, but it's delicious any time of year. You just might find this makes your list of favorite holiday desserts.
—**LAURA SYLVESTER** MECHANICSVILLE, VA

PREP: 30 MIN. • **BAKE:** 70 MIN. + CHILLING
MAKES: 16 SERVINGS

- 1½ cups graham cracker crumbs
- ½ cup finely chopped pecans
- ⅓ cup sugar
- ⅓ cup butter, melted

FILLING

- 3 packages (8 ounces each) cream cheese, softened
- 1½ cups sugar
- 2 cups sour cream
- 1 teaspoon vanilla extract
- ½ teaspoon butter flavoring
- 3 large eggs, lightly beaten
- 1 cup finely chopped pecans

1. In a large bowl, combine cracker crumbs, pecans, sugar and butter; set aside ⅓ cup for topping. Press remaining crumb mixture onto the bottom and 1 in. up the sides of a greased 9-in. springform pan.
2. Place springform pan on a double thickness of heavy-duty foil (about 18 in. square). Securely wrap foil around pan.
3. In a large bowl, beat cream cheese and sugar until smooth. Beat in sour cream, vanilla and butter flavoring. Add eggs; beat on low speed just until combined. Fold in pecans. Pour into crust; sprinkle with reserved crumb mixture. Place springform pan in a large baking pan; add 1 in. of hot water to larger pan.
4. Bake at 325° for 70-80 minutes or until center is almost set. Remove springform pan from water bath. Cool on a wire rack for 10 minutes. Carefully run a knife around edge of pan to loosen; cool 1 hour longer. Refrigerate overnight. Remove sides of pan.

DELICIOUS PUMPKIN BREAD

DELICIOUS PUMPKIN BREAD

An enticing aroma wafts through my house when this tender cakelike bread is in the oven. I bake extra loaves to give as holiday gifts. My friends wait eagerly for it every year.
—**LINDA BURNETT** PRESCOTT, AZ

PREP: 15 MIN. • **BAKE:** 50 MIN. + COOLING
MAKES: 5 MINI LOAVES (8 SLICES EACH)

- 5 large eggs
- 1¼ cups canola oil
- 1 can (15 ounces) solid-pack pumpkin
- 2 cups all-purpose flour
- 2 cups sugar
- 2 packages (3 ounces each) cook-and-serve vanilla pudding mix
- 1 teaspoon baking soda
- 1 teaspoon ground cinnamon
- ½ teaspoon salt

1. In a large bowl, beat eggs. Add oil and pumpkin; beat until smooth. Combine remaining ingredients; gradually beat into pumpkin mixture.
2. Pour batter into five greased 5¾x3x2-in. loaf pans. Bake at 325° for 50-55 minutes or until a toothpick inserted near the center comes out clean. Cool for 10 minutes before removing from pans to wire racks to cool completely.

FREEZE OPTION *Securely wrap and freeze cooled loaves in plastic wrap and foil. To use, thaw loaves at room temperature.*

NOTE *Bread may also be baked in two greased 8x4x2-in. loaf pans for 75-80 minutes.*

FAVORITE BANANA CREAM PIE

Cream pies are my mom's specialty, and this dreamy dessert has a wonderful banana flavor. It looks so pretty topped with almonds...and it cuts easily, too.
—JODI GRABLE SPRINGFIELD, MO

PREP: 10 MIN. • **COOK:** 15 MIN. + CHILLING
MAKES: 8 SERVINGS

- 1 cup sugar
- ¼ cup cornstarch
- ½ teaspoon salt
- 3 cups 2% milk
- 2 large eggs, lightly beaten
- 3 tablespoons butter
- 1½ teaspoons vanilla extract
- 1 pastry shell (9 inches), baked
- 2 large firm bananas
- 1 cup heavy whipping cream, whipped

1. In a large saucepan, combine the sugar, cornstarch, salt and milk until smooth. Cook and stir over medium-high heat until thickened and bubbly. Reduce heat; cook and stir 2 minutes longer. Remove from heat. Stir a small amount of the hot filling into the eggs; return all to pan. Bring to a gentle boil; cook and stir 2 minutes longer.

2. Remove from heat. Gently stir in butter and vanilla. Press plastic wrap onto surface of custard; refrigerate, covered, 30 minutes.

3. Spread half of the custard into the pastry shell. Slice bananas; arrange over the filling. Pour the remaining custard over the bananas. Spread with whipped cream. Refrigerate for 6 hours or overnight.

CHOCOLATE BANANA CREAM PIE

Divide prepared vanilla custard in half. Pour half of the custard into pastry shell. Gently stir 4 ounces melted semisweet chocolate into the remaining custard. Cover and refrigerate both for 30 minutes. Arrange banana slices over the vanilla custard; gently spoon the chocolate custard over top. Proceed as directed.

FAVORITE BANANA CREAM PIE

---

⑤ INGREDIENTS

PUMPKIN-SPICE SUGAR COOKIES

I've been making these quick and easy cookies for over twenty years. They're always the first to go at our annual church bake sale.
—PAULA MARCHESI LENHARTSVILLE, PA

PREP: 20 MIN. + CHILLING
BAKE: 15 MIN./BATCH
MAKES: 4 DOZEN

- 1 cup butter, softened
- 2 cups sugar
- 2 large eggs
- 2¾ cups all-purpose flour
- 2 tablespoons pumpkin pie spice
  Cinnamon sugar, optional

1. Cream butter and sugar until light and fluffy. Beat in the eggs. In another bowl, whisk the flour and pie spice; gradually beat into creamed mixture. Divide dough in half. Shape each into a disk; wrap in plastic. Refrigerate 1 hour or until firm enough to roll.

2. Preheat oven to 350°. On a lightly floured surface, roll each portion of dough to ¼-in. thickness. Cut with a floured 2½-in. round cookie cutter. Place 1 in. apart on ungreased baking sheets. If desired, sprinkle with cinnamon sugar.

3. Bake 12-14 minutes or until edges are light brown. Cool on pans for 1 minute, then remove to wire racks.

FREEZE OPTION *Transfer wrapped disks to a resealable plastic freezer bag; freeze. To use, thaw dough in refrigerator overnight or until soft enough to roll. Prepare and bake cookies as directed.*

✳

TEST KITCHEN TIP The best tool to prevent a "skin" from forming on custards, puddings and cream-pie fillings is plastic wrap. Immediately after making the custard, place a piece of plastic wrap on the surface, smoothing it so that it makes full contact. It's the exposure to the air that hardens the surface and creates the skin!

**PUMPKIN-SPICE
SUGAR COOKIES**

GENERAL INDEX

ALPHABETICAL INDEX